With
best wishes
from Colin Smith

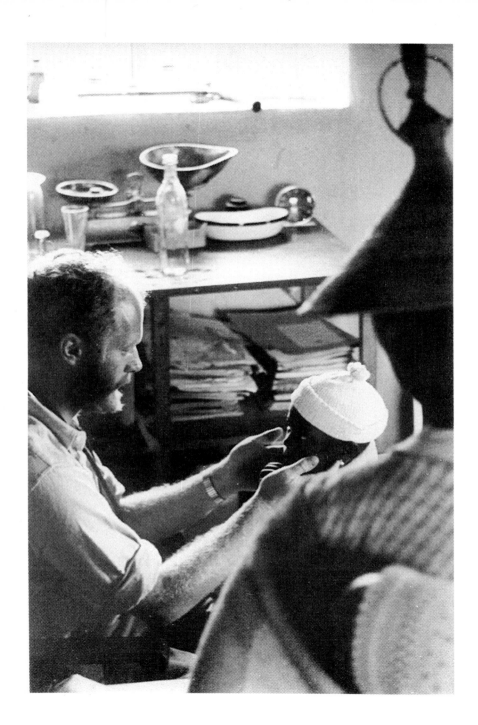

GREEN MOUNTAIN DOCTOR

Memoirs of a government medical officer in Basutoland in the nineteen sixties

Colin Smith

Published by
Colin Smith
6 Shorts Lane
Beaminster
Dorset
DT8 3BD
1st September 2000

ISBN 0-9538895-0-5

Front cover photograph and page 2 by Karl de Haan
Back cover photograph by Innis McAllister
Map of Qachas's Nek by Captain Shortt-Smith BMP
Drawings by Colin Smith
Photographs by Colin & Celia Smith
Printed and bound in Great Britain
by
Creeds the Printers
Broadoak
Bridport
Dorset
DT6 5NL

PREFACE

It may be that I have not been able to remember the actual words spoken by people forty years ago, and that I have therefore had to construct a dialogue out of the sort of thing people would have said. I have also moved the incidents around in time, but they all actually occurred as I have described them, as my letters to my mother and father, which I still have, testify.

The people I have described were real, and have their real names.

The incidents do not always show me in a good light, and I hope that any Basuto (or more correctly Basotho) who read this will forgive me my mis-perceptions and sometimes dangerous lack of knowledge and skill. There were many excellent "bush surgeons" who would have done much better than I did, but they were somewhere else.

Though the mountains were green in patches, this story is about a green doctor, not a green mountain.

I would like to thank David Ormerod in particular for reading and commenting on the stories as I unfolded them to him.

I dedicate this story to Celia, my constant companion, now as then.

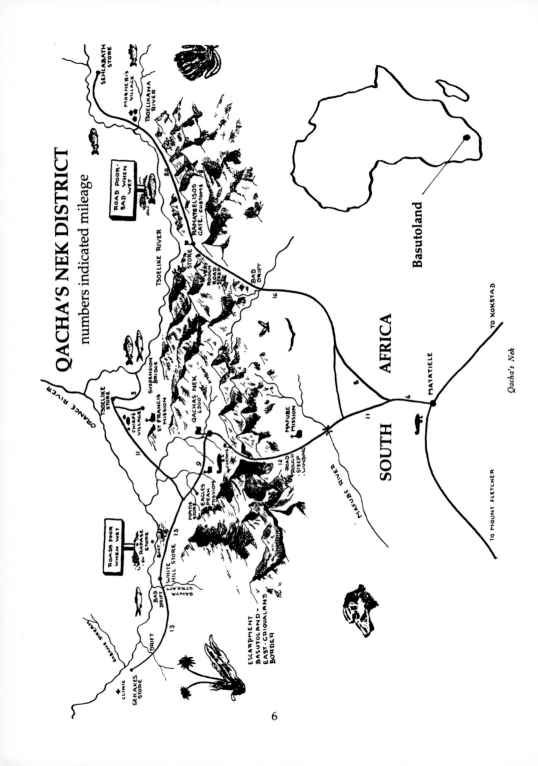

QACHA'S NEK DISTRICT
numbers indicated mileage

ORANGE RIVER

SEHLABATH STORE

MOSHESH'S VILLAGE

TSOELIKANA RIVER

ROAD POOR - BAD WHEN WET

20

RAMATSELISOS GATE, CUSTOMS

8

TSOELIKE RIVER

ROUGH ROAD STEEP

STORE

BAD DRIFT

16

TSOELIKE STORE

5

SUSPENSION BRIDGE

CHIEFS VILLAGE

ST FRANCIS MISSION

QACHAS NEK 6300'

11

9

MAFUBE MISSION

EAGLES PEAK MISSION

CUSTOMS

12

ROAD ROUGH STEEP WINDING

MATYIS STORE

ROADS POOR WHEN WET

RAPASE STORE

BAD DRIFT

BOAT

13

WHITE HILL STORE

GANYA STREAM

ESCARPMENT - BASUTOLAND - EAST - GRIQUALAND BORDER

13

DRIFT

GANYA STREAM

CLINIC

SEKAKES STORE

MAFUBE RIVER

SOUTH AFRICA

8

11

6

MATATIELE

Basutoland

TO KOKSTAD

TO MOUNT FLETCHER

Qacha's Nek

6

CONTENTS

Trek Airways - an elderly aeroplane - recalling the experiences and feelings - people - idealism and other agendas - forty years on - that's how it was .

INTRODUCTION

It is a curious thing, writing forty years after the events, musing upon the person you were at that time, looking back through the long glass tube of your mind at both the inside and outside of that person, so familiar yet in many ways so different.

Most of my early upbringing took place during the Second World War at Branksome-Hilders, my father's boarding Preparatory school for boys near Hindhead in Surrey. Because of the war many boys stayed on for the holidays, as their parents were away fighting, but I remember this as a very happy time. The school was surrounded by dense woodland, where we could climb, build huts, fight mock battles and test ourselves in risky situations; we were all determined to be heroes. Dogfights roared and stuttered overhead, while we cheered our airmen on. During one such fight a Messerschmidt's tail fell close by and we bore it triumphantly back and leant it against a tree. I was rather hoping the Germans might invade, as I was going to let them have it with my air rifle when they appeared at the bottom of the lawn.

After the war the boys all went home during the holidays and I was left mooning around in the dreadful emptiness of the place. Fortunately the school had an extensive but formless library which my father had bought as a job lot in an auction and this was a source of great pleasure and solace to me. I devoured adventure stories, especially those of Percy F. Westerman, Jules Verne, Rider Haggard and John Buchan, and I developed a vivid imaginative picture of the world outside, most particularly of Africa, where I longed to go, one day.

I was very keen on the Scouts, and took the Law and Promise very seriously. I thoroughly enjoyed the camping, the learning how to do things with ropes, and the climbing of trees and crawling through the undergrowth, that it involved. I was intensely patriotic. Our Scoutmaster was a gentle Evangelical, who was able to conjure Christ in our minds, and whose quiet Christian teaching lives with me still.

Despite knowing that I would end up in Heaven one day, I was often fearful, and kept setting myself frightening tasks. These usually involved climbing something, in order to overcome this fearfulness. There was a wonderful selection of trees to climb at Branksome, varying between

11

easy and impossible. To be a hundred feet above the ground in one of the huge conifers, enclosing the entire trunk in one hand as the wind swayed me to and fro, looking down on the buildings and grounds, kindled a feeling that was near to ecstasy. Once, when I was eleven or so, I climbed a cypress tree by the dining room, stepped across onto the gutter, walked gingerly up the slope of the roof and clambered awhile amongst the gullies and chimneys, finally finding a way back into the house through a dormer window. Success in such enterprises solved my problem by making me feel bold, but generated a sense of superiority which made me unsympathetic towards those who did not dare to do such things. I loved to scrap and wrestle with whoever was willing.

Later I went to Charterhouse, a boarding school for older boys. It was an austere Victorian Gothic place on a windy hilltop, where we were taught that with our privileges came responsibilities, and that we might well end up in positions of leadership. My teachers had little respect for my academic ability, even doubting whether I would pass the School Certificate, as the GCSE was then called, so they were duly astonished when I managed to win a scholarship to Trinity College at Oxford to study Medicine. I had decided to be a doctor when I was four years old, as I wanted to possess the magical power to make things right, that Dr Holmes, our dapper little GP with his gold watch chain and pin-striped suit, could exert.

So it was a conventional enough middle class upbringing, if rather lacking in the feminine touch, but with various other influences to leaven the lump. My father was a Yorkshireman of strong and thoughtful opinions, who felt that it was generally your duty to make up your own mind about things, and that what most people thought, or wanted to do, was probably wrong. He told us that should be prepared to "swim against the tide" of general opinion if we felt that it was right to do so.

From all these influences I came to understand that my own instincts and yearnings were suspect, and thoughtfulness and logic would often countermand them. There was a continuous conflict between not only what I *wanted* to do and what I *ought* to do, but between who I wanted to *be* and who I ought to *be*.

My father's world view reflected his schoolmasterly attitude. He saw the world as a giant school playground, with countries and regimes acting as schoolchildren, with all the same potential for kindness and cruelty, generosity and bullying, and believed that they would respond to the same sorts of remedy of ethical strictness. Conflict was inevitable, but the defeated enemy should be treated with generosity and magnanimity. Hence despite having flown in the Royal Flying Corps in the First World War, he was profoundly opposed to the Treaty of Versailles, which humiliated the defeated Germans.

He bought an ancient yacht just after the next war and took us on exciting, rather ill-thought out, and occasionally hazardous adventures on both sides of the Channel, from Holland to the Isles of Scilly. Apart from being frequently unsure of our position, we were dismasted once and eventually sank after striking the Manacle rocks, off the Lizard peninsula, but the boat was fished out and our erratic progress carried on.

My mother found all this manliness a bit daunting and was often fearful of the consequences of our activities. She made an excellent Headmaster's wife, though found it laid great burdens on her which sometimes seemed to wear her down. My elder brother David was a great hero of mine, and I used to trail around behind him admiringly. This irritated him, and he did his best to ignore me until I was about sixteen, when I held him as he nearly fell of the parapet of Fort Grosnez in Alderney. I was especially proud of him when he went on to fight in Korea in the Royal Artillery. His letters home made it sound like a jolly romp, but I think he was profoundly disturbed by it.

My parents were fascinated by stories of personal courage and adventurousness, such as those of Mallory and Irvine on Everest, and Shackleton and Scott in the Antarctic.

There was a lot of military activity at Charterhouse in those days, and I learned how to command a platoon of cadets in various tactical situations, and how to fire, dismantle and even instruct upon the Bren light machine gun. I was joint winner of the Gonne cup for marksmanship with the first world war Lee Enfield rifles with which the cadet corps was provided, and I only wished I had been old enough to fight in the war, as I felt I would certainly have survived as a hero. On one glorious day I was promoted to Senior Under Officer so that I could command a guard of honour of a hundred cadets when Lord Louis Mountbatten came to unveil a memorial to the Chindit General, Orde Wingate.

Running rather counter to all this, I wanted to sing; I could sense some kind of perfection in singing in harmony which drew me on. So I joined the choir, to the derision of most of my schoolmates, who thought it sissy, and I loved it and still do. I also took up the flute, and set out on a lifetime of musical enjoyment. I was generally happy and cheerful, but like most boys of that age hated making a fool of myself. I solved this problem brilliantly by acting the goat a lot of the time, so that no-one could tell whether I was making a fool of myself by mistake or on purpose.

I was almost useless at sports involving balls, which was very bad for my prestige, though I later showed some promise in sailing, fencing, rowing and climbing.

13

My time at Oxford was marvellous. I imbibed the mediaeval atmosphere with the greatest delight and learned the basics of Medicine, and dissected my first corpse. The complete absence of any sort of person from these pathetic hulks confirmed my belief in the soul. We seemed to have to work harder than other students, but between whiles I sang in the Bach Choir, rowed indifferently on the Isis, went to church a lot, learned how to fire a 25 pounder howitzer in the Artillery section of the Territorial Army, and climbed to the top of the Radcliffe Camera one memorable night, leaving my boat club tie attached to the lightning conductor to prove it.

I especially enjoyed the riotous assemblies of Bump Supper and Guy Fawkes nights. I joined the University Mountaineering Club, bought a nylon climbing rope and a pair of heavily nailed boots. We climbed amongst the rocks and gullies of North Wales in the holidays, and later I bought an Army surplus ice axe and some crampons, and graduated to the Swiss Alps.

The time came to experience real patients, and I moved on to Guy's Hospital for my clinical training. Parts of Guy's were still propped up by massive beams, a legacy from the Blitz, and the hospital was proud to have shared the risks of that terrible time with the rest of the East Enders. This gave rise to a rather gung-ho attitude, as they liked to drop students into the deep end to get on with it as far as possible, especially in the Casualty Department, which suited me. Prior to Guy's I had been educated in an almost entirely male environment, but for the first time in my life I was surrounded by nubile young women, some of whom I found disturbingly attractive.

The Oxford final examinations were ahead of those in London and I managed to fit in three months as a supernumerary Medical Officer on the *Frubel Clementina*, a 3,000 ton banana boat sailing between Antwerp and the Belgian Congo; this gave me my first real experience of Africa, and whetted my appetite for more.

On my return I took up my post as a Junior House Physician at Guy's, which was quite an honour. The Guy's consultants of those days were generally courteous and helpful, and it was a pleasure to try and please them, though for some reason one of them disliked me intensely, and I came to dislike him in return. He dished my chance of a second six months job there despite the support I received from the other consultants.

In the event this tiff was of little importance as I had meanwhile decided to take a year off to join Christopher Ellis as Mate and Medical Officer on a cruise around the North Atlantic under sail on his Bristol Channel Pilot Cutter *Theodora*. I was twenty five and fed up with being educated, and I had grown my first serious beard. We set off from Camper and Nicholson's yard at Southampton on October 20 1958, for a wonderful, romantic but sometimes frightening voyage. When far from land there was always a groundswell of fear waiting to burst into consciousness when something looked as if it might go wrong, so the yacht proved to be another vehicle for overcoming such fears.

When we reached the West Indies I worked for three months as a house surgeon in Barbados under Jack Leacock, a brilliant but occasionally manic surgeon, and was involved in dealing with a wide spectrum of diseases, accidents, gynaecological problems and disasters which would not normally have come my way. I learned a lot about improvising and how to deal with the unexpected..

Fortunately at this point Celia joined the cruise and entered my life, though at first I ignored her completely, and she thought me arrogant and rude. Actually I was pining for an inaccessible young woman and had no eyes for any other female at that time. I began to notice Celia as the cruise progressed up the Eastern seaboard of the USA, and by the time we reached England again I was in awe of her intelligence and fearlessness in often frightening situations. A gale in mid Atlantic with water crashing all over the place strips off pretences and I became powerfully attracted to her, though drew back from pursuing the relationship when we returned home, as I had to finish my pre-registration year before I was a fully fledged doctor.

During three months as an Orthopaedic House Surgeon at Whipp's Cross Hospital in Leytonstone I learned a lot about dealing with broken bones. In the next six months of Surgery, I learned how to get in and out of an abdomen and various other tricks of the trade.

My National Service had been delayed until my training was finished, and I had decided to go to Basutoland as a government Medical Officer for three years as this was a permitted alternative. National Service was cancelled before I was due to go, but I wanted to go anyway, as the books I had read as a boy made it sound fascinating, and there might be scope for all kinds of adventure.

The hint of danger and instability, which had been brought into focus by the recent massacre of 69 black Africans by the increasingly despised South African Police at Sharpeville, only made me keener. I would be perfectly safe, anyway. Surely no-one in their right mind would shoot a doctor who was trying to look after casualties from whatever side.

So there I was: romantic, a bit arrogant, with a sense of Christian destiny, physically and mentally tough, cheerful to the point of silliness at times, but with a wider range of medical and surgical knowledge and skills than was usual for a doctor at that stage of his career, though nowhere near enough for the tasks that lay ahead.

My mother took me to Woolworth's in Haslemere and made me buy two plastic plates, cups and saucers and knives, forks and spoons, and various other useful household items. In due course these basic necessities were packed into two tea chests and hoisted aboard the *Athlone Castle*, bound for Cape Town.

Though I have no recollection of the event, my friend and colleague Tony Trafford told me that at some time before setting sail I had said to him in deeply serious tones after a couple of glasses of wine: "Tony; it's either Africa or a woman!"

I was wrong. In the end I achieved both.

Theodora

CHAPTER 1
EARLY DAYS

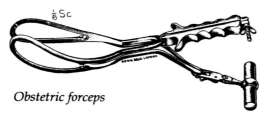

Obstetric forceps

The baby was dead, the head low and the mother was exhausted when she was brought in. Carefully I slid the forceps either side of the baby's head, locked them and leaned back. I had never applied forceps unsupervised before, though I had attended lectures and seen them demonstrated while a student at Guy's. One thing I knew for certain was that if they were carefully applied and the handles locked, they could not possibly come off.

* * *

I had been looking forward to going to Basutoland for several months, though I had no idea where it was, apart from a vague notion that it was north of the Limpopo river. In fact it was a thousand miles further south. My first impressions of the little kingdom were very favourable and I felt that I had three interesting and exciting years ahead of me.

Leribe, a small town a couple of hours dusty drive north of Maseru, was my first posting in Basutoland. Geoff Wilkinson, a tall, rangy, pipe smoking South African was the Medical Officer at that time. He and his wife and children made me welcome in their low golden stone house with a magnificent view of the distant Maluti mountains.

"We're off on holiday in a couple of day's time, so I'd better show you how to do a Caesar", he said, after showing me round the hospital. "You never know when you might need to do one. As it happens I will be doing one this afternoon. You can give me a hand."

We scrubbed up and I watched goggle eyed as he made a long vertical incision into the middle of the mother's distended abdomen. The abdominal wall was incredibly thin.

"You mustn't make too deep an incision, as the baby's only a little way in, and it looks bad if you cut the baby."

He made a similar incision into the front of the uterus, and put down his scalpel. He plunged in his hand and hauled the bloodied baby out by its two feet, holding it upside down for a moment.

At his request I clipped, tied and cut the umbilical cord, which still snaked back into the wound, and he handed the baby to a nurse who was standing by. Then he schlooped out the placenta and the rest of the cord, closed the uterus and later the abdominal wall with large, deep sutures, and finally closed the skin with fine silk.

"The big stitches staunch the bleeding and the little ones make her look tidy. She has so much spare tummy now that everything goes back nicely. Quite simple; saves lives. Most other things can wait a bit, but you have to get on with a Caesar. Now you know what to do, that shouldn't be a problem."

It was so quick, and so matter-of-fact. The problem was that I had never done anything like that before, and I seriously doubted if I would have the nerve if the occasion arose, so I said nothing and hoped that no-one would be admitted in obstructed labour before he returned.

Two days later the Wilkinsons left on their holiday. When they had gone, I surveyed my new domain. The hospital was clean and sunny, with about sixty beds, and a simple operating theatre. It was well supplied with Basuto nurses and other staff. It even had a real sister with a white uniform and a proper sister's cap that spread out behind her head. Everyone was extremely friendly. The little town nearby still had the fort from the time of the gun wars, and the rondavel where General Gordon had stayed while negotiating with the angry Basuto in the 1870s. From the stoep I could see rugged *kranzes* rising out of the dusty plains, and the blue-grey peaks of the mountains lining the eastern horizon.

So I was on my own, and a few days later was facing my first serious test, to deliver a dead baby in order to save a mother's life.

Obstetric forceps are beautifully designed for their purpose, which is gently to stretch the mother's birth canal while protecting the baby's head between two blades, which constitute a cage of steel, and allowing it to descend. The curves of the forceps are so graceful and the steel of such quality, that they take up almost no room between the baby's head and the mother's vagina. The blades are inserted one at a time. I laid the handle of the first blade on the unconscious mother's abdomen, slid it into her vagina and lowered the handle gently so that the blade slipped

19

snugly round the baby's cheek. Then I slipped the other blade round the baby's other cheek and locked the handles together. Once they are locked together you may be unable to deliver the baby, but they cannot come off. So we were told when we learned our obstetrics.

But they did come off. I reapplied them several times, but every time that I started to draw the baby out, they jumped off. I looked at the shining steel forceps and tried to work out what on earth could be going on.

I was beginning to get alarmed. The mother was exhausted and as she had been under ether for some time, a Caesar would be hazardous at this stage, even if I dared to try. The dead baby had to be delivered somehow or the mother would die as well. There was no-one to help or give advice. Apart from a nurse and the dispenser dropping the ether on the mask, there was no-one else there at all.

* * *

I had only been in Basutoland for a few days. My last job, the second after qualifying, had been as the lowest form of medical life, a house surgeon at Whipp's Cross Hospital in Leytonstone. It was a good job, and I had learned much more than usual in such a junior post, including how to open and close an abdomen, but I had never come across a situation anything like this. With no-one to ask or share the responsibility; I felt terribly alone. Nobody else there seemed worried; the problem was entirely mine.

I looked despairingly round the operating room for inspiration, but there was little to be found in the grey cement walls with four or five glass fronted cabinets along them. This was awful; I felt the fear rising in my stomach. Some way had to be found to deliver this baby. Something caught my eye. "What are those instruments in that cabinet over there?" I asked, "Bring them over here."

My eyes had not deceived me. These were the archaic instruments illustrated in the back pages of Gibberd's masterly *Short Textbook of Midwifery*. The pictures had stuck in my mind because of the horror of their implication; that it might be necessary to dismember a dead baby in the womb. No student was taught how they were to be used, because with modern techniques they were no longer necessary.

I made up my mind, glad to see a way forward, awful though it was. There was nothing else to be done. "Boil them up", I said

I waited between the mother's elevated legs with my gloved hands clasped in front of my chest until the boiled and quenched instruments were brought to me on a sterile towel, about ten minutes later. I could feel the baby's anterior fontanelle easily, as it was only a couple of inches up the vagina. I picked up the perforator, which was like a long handled pair of scissors, with short blades sharpened on the outside, and thrust the point through the fontanelle into the baby's skull.

There was a rush of clear fluid; a pint or so. So that was why the forceps had jumped off! They were only grasping the top part of a huge collapsed head. I replaced the perforator on the towel and picked up the craniotomy forceps, which were like a pair of long, curved pliers, inserted the shorter jaw into the aperture in the baby's skull, and drew out the remains of the poor little hydrocephalic child.

The afterbirth came down easily but was followed in turn by a rush of blood. Once again I had never done this before, but I had been told about it and it had stuck in my mind. Placing my right clenched fist up the vagina and my left cupped hand on the mothers abdomen, I squeezed the womb firmly between them and the bleeding stopped immediately. This was what was known dryly in the text book as *bi-manual compression of the uterus.*

I mentally blessed Gibberd's wonderfully lucid style, and his straightforward explanations of what had to be done under certain circumstances. The fact that the textbook, unlike most, was a delight to read had meant that these dramatic manoeuvres had lodged firmly in my mind, even though I would never have to use them. Or so I had thought at the time.

After this baptism of fire, I walked shakily back to the great, bare tin-roofed stone house I had been allocated by the Basutoland government. It was far bigger than I needed and hardly furnished. I threw myself into an arm chair and stared a while into the darkness of the huge sitting room with the events of the last couple of hours whirling through my head. I was not used to this degree of solitude.

"What would you like for supper, Morena?" asked my Basuto maid. I had absolutely no idea, as I had never had to make that sort of decision before. In the past I simply stuffed myself with whatever was provided by somebody, so sorting out what had to be bought at the market to make the food was quite beyond me, and I wasn't getting much to eat as a consequence. I partially solved the problem by hanging round people's houses at supper time until they invited me in.

So perhaps it was not entirely surprising that my mind turned to Celia, who had sailed across the Atlantic with me and five others in Chris Ellis' pilot cutter, *Theodora*, the previous year. She could steer a good course in a following sea, was never fazed by the most frightening weather, and didn't suffer from the various unpredictable moods that seemed to afflict most young women of my acquaintance. It came as something of a revelation that though our paths had diverged somewhat while I was

Celia

completing my house jobs, I was lonely and in love. I felt strongly that this love had been smouldering all along and that it took this particular situation to allow the scales to fall from my eyes. Sometimes I wonder if chronic hunger played a part in my thinking at that time.

My mind was made up. Basutoland was no place for a bachelor. Something had to be done. Suddenly revitalised, I grovelled in one of the two tea chests that contained all my belongings, and triumphantly pulled out a zipped writing case. I opened the case, took out a blue aerogramme form, sat down by the window and after gnawing the pen for some time wrote:

Dear Celia,

I am enjoying myself doctoring out here though it is very different from England; there is plenty to keep me busy.

You'd love it here; it's a fascinating little country with dusty plains and distant mountains and practically everybody on horseback all the time. I was wondering if you would come out and join me? The only snag is that if you want the government to pay the fare you would have to marry me.

I don't have much to offer but it would be fun and I could at least give you a fair amount of affection and I know you wouldn't be bored.

With love

from

Colin.

I read it through. Not very romantic, but I didn't want to put any pressure on Celia, and I wanted to armour myself against rejection. It was more of an experiment really, to see how my thoughts would look in writing if I were to send something of the sort. I didn't have to send it anyway, it was just an idea.

Then, by some curious trick of the mind, I forgot all about it. The next day, without thinking or really being aware of what I was doing, I folded over the little tags on the aerogramme, licked them and stuck it up.

When I arrived at the hospital for the morning round I accidentally left it on the end of sister's desk with the other outgoing mail. When I returned to sister's office for coffee after seeing all the patients, the desk was clear. The mail had all gone.

For the first time I realised the awe-inspiring significance of what I had done. But I quickly dismissed the whole matter from my mind. The fuse was lit and what would be, would be. There was plenty else to think about for the time being.

Who could I cadge supper from tonight?

CHAPTER 2
THE WEDDING

The house at Qacha's Nek

Gideon Pott, the District Commissioner of Leribe, was a true English gentleman. Handsome, moustached, always perfectly groomed, he had an excellent seat on a horse. Except for the view from the French windows, his residence could have been in one of the more prosperous parts of Surrey. *Country Life* magazines were elegantly fanned out on the drawing room table and fine china and family photos were carefully placed about.

He had several horses in his stable, and rather rashly offered to lend me one, a handsome thoroughbred, so that I could explore the District. I swallowed my nerves and willingly accepted. I was getting the impression that in Basutoland nerves were unacceptable. In any case this gave me a chance to show off the wonderful military riding boots I had bought second hand at Moss Bros. in Covent Garden for just such an occasion.

I had noticed a rocky *kranz* standing out of the plain several miles away, with a plateau on top which ended in a vertical cliff several hundred feet high. It looked as if it might have a gentler approach from the other side, so I set off on this beautiful horse to find out. Though the plain looked flat, there were all sorts of hazard between me and my destination, including a winding, mud-coloured river forty or fifty feet wide. We waded in. The horse was evidently used to this sort of thing, but I was not, and the water began to creep up my splendid boots. I was about to try to throw myself off and swim alongside, when the water level began to fall again, and we emerged streaming on the other side.

When we finally reached the *kranz* I had to dismount and lead the horse between the rocks up the last steep climb, but eventually we reached the top. I remounted and we walked to the edge of the cliff. I felt that I would have cut a fine figure silhouetted against the sky as I peered back toward the camp, if there had been anyone there to see.

* * *

I was just beginning to settle into my new life when I was recalled to the capital, Maseru. I was to be transferred to Qacha's Nek, an obscure district somewhere on the other side of the territory. Nobody seemed to know anything about it. It seemed that Qacha was some long-forgotten chieftain, and Nek means a pass between two peaks.

The territory was so mountainous that the only way to get about was by one of the handful of light aircraft belonging to Basutair, our miniature airline. Our first attempt to fly across the snow-capped Maluti mountains from the airport at Maseru in a little, four-seater Tri-pacer, was a failure, as the high peaks were shrouded in cloud. As there was no way to fly through the clouds, we had to return to the airfield. The next day we boarded the little Tri-pacer again, and as we approached the mountain tops, a tunnel roofed by cloud appeared between two peaks, through which we were able to scuttle into the sunlight beyond.

The weather closed in again on the other side of the last ridge; and we flew into a snowstorm that completely obscured the countryside. Of the landing strip there was no sign, but that didn't seem to bother Vossie, who was flying the plane that day. After a while the long corrugated iron roof of a Roman Catholic mission station appeared through the whirling flakes, and we flew close above it.

"No need to worry. We just have to point the plane along the roof and you will see the end of the strip ahead of us," Vossie assured me, easing back on the throttle and hauling the lever that operated the flaps up a notch as he lined us up.

For a moment the little plane seemed poised, floating in grey nothingness, but then, sure enough, the edge of a cliff appeared ahead.

As Vossie pulled the flaps right up the cliff fell away close beneath us. He throttled back and the little plane settled gently into a foot of snow, trundled for a while and drew up by the shack which served as an air terminal. When the motor had stopped we climbed out and the cold hit us after the heated cabin of the plane.

"Climb in, *Morena ngaka*, I have come to take you to your new home". A cheerful Basuto policeman, dressed in khaki, with the side of his trek hat pinned up, was standing by a Land Rover behind the shack. We climbed in and he drove us the mile or so into the camp, as it was still called in memory of the pioneering days of the nineteenth century. Clutching my small suitcase I was delivered to a driveway between two hedges. My two tea chests of possessions were to follow later.

"Up there, *Morena*. That is to be your house," said the policemen, and drove away. Rather dazed, I walked up the drive with Vossie, who was hoping for a cup of something hot, and climbed the steps to the *stoep* in front of the house. I could see that it was made of stone, with a red iron roof; a smaller version of the house in Leribe, but that was about all. I turned round to look across the valley, but could see nothing but snowflakes, dark against the grey sky. I had always thought Africa was a hot dry place, but clearly this wasn't the case in Qacha's Nek. It was very cold.

I knocked on the door and a greying middle-aged man wrapped in a pullover topped by a grey cardigan invited me into the little dining room. A fire of curious looking balls (which turned out later to be a mixture of coal dust and cow dung) glowed in the grate.

"You must be Colin Smith. Hello, Vossie, any news from the metropolis?" he said as he shook my hand. "Shut the door if you don't mind. Not an easy house to keep warm. Breakfast anybody? A message came over the police radio that you were on your way." He was evidently very pleased to see us. "Usually I do a round at the hospital first thing and then have something to eat, but today is different. Nothing much going on just now, thanks to the weather. Take a seat anyway. I'm George Parker by the way; and this is my wife Sylvia. As soon as it brightens up a bit I'll take you round the hospital, and then we'll be off and it's over to you."

The storm passed and the little valley was flooded with sunlight. It was astonishingly beautiful. We were one of a cluster of low houses along the side of a valley surrounded by glittering peaks, and the whole valley and the low hills around it were blanketed white. The branches of a little copse of conifers behind the house were laden with snow. This was a magical place. Vossie stayed behind to supply Sylvia with the latest gossip and George and I went to have a look at the hospital.

This was not so magical. The hospital consisted basically of two dung plastered wards of about twenty beds each, one male and one female, and a small operating theatre. Medical, clean and septic surgical and obstetric cases were all mixed together which seemed frankly dangerous. There was an incredible washing machine with a perforated drum which revolved in a trough of water kept boiling by a fire beneath. It was turned with a large crank handle. In addition there was a modern building for patients with tuberculosis and a tiny mortuary. There was a small breeze block house for lepers just outside the camp.

"Not ideal, I agree, but there are plans afoot to build new maternity and children's wards, and to do the place up generally," said George, "and the staff are tremendous. Let's pop across the road and have a look at the dispensary and X-ray machine."

The tour of inspection did not take long."Goodbye and good luck!" George and Sylvia and their baggage were off as soon as the plane could fly again.

As the snow turned to slush the magnitude of what I had taken on began to sink in. Fortunately there was so much to do that it didn't sink in too far. The first thing was to explore the house, so I went out onto the long stone *stoep* under the overhanging roof, so that I could come in again. I had to open a wire mesh screen before I could open the front door, presumably a defence against flying insects, though it was hard to believe that insects would be a problem at 6,500 feet. Maybe when these houses were built, flyscreens were standard all over the British Empire, regardless of climate. This house was clearly designed for the tropics.

As I entered the little hall the dining room was to the left, and the main bedroom opposite, with a marvellous view of Mount Sauer across the valley through the sash window. There was a spare bedroom behind the dining room, and the kitchen behind that. A door led out of the bedroom into what looked like a small garage, with a bath and lavatory in it. There was a drawing room in a separate wing, but it was closed off for the winter. It was very quiet.

Elsie, a quiet, middle-aged Mosuto woman who lived in a hut at the back of the house, was going to feed and look after me at home, and the dispensers and nurses were going to introduce me to the staff and show me the ropes. It dawned on me that I was going to be extremely busy. Furthermore as a Government Medical Officer I was going to have to be a specialist in everything, from surgery to sewage.

In addition to all this there was a wedding to arrange, as Celia would be over in a couple of weeks. I was anxious that it would be memorable and well organised occasion. There was a morning suit to hire, a cake to order, rings to buy and invitations to send out.

27

An expatriate wedding at Qacha's Nek hadn't happened within living memory, and the women of the dusty little community were galvanised into action. The date was to be the 10th of December in St Barnabas' little church, a couple of hundred yards along the stony road. Father Michael Hardy C.R. with his huge black beard, who was usually to be seen on horseback under a decrepit slouch hat, carrying the consecrated bread and wine to remote villages, would marry us.

Celia had been sharing a flat in South Kensington with her cousin, the young actress Sarah Long, when my letter arrived. She was working as assistant to the fiction editor of the *Evening News* at the time. She found my letter a bit odd, and it threw her into such a mental turmoil that she became quite difficult to live with. Eventually Sarah took her in hand and said "If you don't marry him, I will!" and that helped Celia make up her mind. After all, though the letter wasn't very romantic she already knew me pretty well, and had a fair idea what she would be in for.

It seemed that I had shown more low cunning in the letter than I realised with my conscious mind, because part of my brain had calculated that Celia was far more likely to say "yes" to a letter from Basutoland, than if I had asked her from Haslemere, a mere ten miles away from her family home in Dunsfold. Whatever her reasoning, to my delight, she wrote back to me, accepting my proposal.

She had just had a wonderful twenty-first birthday party on a river boat on the Thames, and was thoroughly enjoying her first job. Life was good, but having made up her mind to join me, she and her parents soon made the necessary arrangements. Within a few weeks she, accompanied by my mother and my Uncle Eric, were at Heathrow airport boarding one of the new jet-propelled Comet airliners, *en route* for Johannesburg.

The situation was rather different in Basutoland. The journey from Qacha's Nek to Johannesburg was more complicated than the one from Dunsfold to Heathrow. Firstly, long before Celia boarded the plane back in England, I was given a lift in the medical Land Rover down the spectacular track to the nearest railhead at Matatiele. This was thirty five miles away at the bottom of the escarpment in the Republic of South Africa. It was a pretty little town, well supplied with shops and a huge store. I found a beautiful engagement ring there, a large pale opal surrounded by diamond chips, so I bought it, and a wedding ring. I found a cake shop too, where they would make me a three-tier wedding cake.

As I boarded the train to Pietermaritzburg I began to feel a bit peculiar, and from there on the journey became increasingly blurred. I must have picked up some sort of flu, because I was beginning to burn up with fever and everything was becoming strange and dreamy. I managed to catch the train from Pietermaritzburg to Johannesburg, but the rest of the journey was a bit of a nightmare. The narrow gauge trains were extremely slow and it seemed to go on for ever.

Eventually I arrived, and my Uncle Bert picked me up at the station and drove me home to his bungalow in Sandringham, where Celia had already arrived and was being fussed over by Auntie Mary and their two girls, Heather and Hazel. Celia was all flushed and eager at the start of her new adventure, but I felt awful. I could scarcely raise a welcoming grin, which must have been rather disconcerting for her after flying ten thousand miles to be with me. I made a supreme effort and managed to smile when I presented her with the engagement ring, as I was afraid she would take the next plane back to England after such a reception from her husband to be.

The train journey back wasn't much fun either. I was still feeling pretty terrible, and though we were allowed to share the shiny green leather upholstered couchette by day, as darkness began to fall a fierce female guard appeared and interrogated us. When we admitted that we weren't married she firmly put us in separate compartments. At one station the lady Celia was sharing with thrust a baby in her arms and disappeared into the gloom in search of a drink of water. To Celia's alarm the train then pulled out of the station before the woman returned. After ten minutes it reversed back into the station, to her and the mother's great relief.

When we eventually arrived at Matatiele, the Police Land Rover met us for the thirty five mile grind back up the escarpment to Qacha's Nek, and it was with a huge sense of relief that we finally staggered into what was to be our new home on the side of the valley. Elsie welcomed us and soon produced tea. Celia was entranced with her new house, especially the cast iron cooking stove, of incredible antiquity, inscribed "Magic No 1", but soon it was time to walk across the fifty yards or so to the District Commissioner's house where she was to stay. It was two whole weeks to the wedding and it would have been quite improper if we had spent the night under the same roof before we were married.

Stephen Howard, the District Commissioner, his rather cynical wife June, and their teenage daughter Fleur, kindly put Celia up in the guest rondavel in their garden, so her luggage was taken round there. The Residency was only a short distance away from my house, through some scrub and rough grass, so every morning she would walk across before breakfast and spend the day with me.

A few evenings later the cloud base had become so low that the whole valley was shrouded in mist. We were sitting at the dining table waiting for Elsie to bring in one of her enormous but rather tough omelettes for supper, when we noticed a strong smell of burning. At first we thought something must be burning in the kitchen, but nothing was wrong there. When we threw open the sash window and peered into the foggy darkness, we found that the smell was stronger outside.

"It's coming from the Residency!" I cried and chased off towards a crackling noise in the murk with Celia in hot pursuit. Indeed the Residency was well ablaze, so I ran off to the police station and told the policeman on duty. He must have telephoned the gaol, as within a short time a gang of cheerful convicts appeared, and Celia found herself in a chain of them passing buckets of water in a desperate and ultimately fruitless attempt to douse the fire.

"Things were never like this in Surrey" she thought as she hoisted yet another pail of water to the grinning convict, with his striped jersey and red Tam o' Shanter in the smoky murk; "This must be the real Africa!"

The next day revealed that while the Residency, and with it one of the bridesmaid's dresses, had been destroyed, Celia's dress and wedding accoutrements had survived in the guest rondavel. So June and her friends set to to make another dress for little red-haired Foxy Lee, the Police Officer's daughter, as the wedding was only ten days away.

Fortunately for me, the little community of expatriate wives took pity on me and bustled cheerfully around organising the reception, which was a huge weight off my mind. I had managed to order the cake, buy the rings, hire a morning suit and send out the invitations despite being somewhat distracted by trying to run the hospital, which would have been extremely difficult but for the loyalty and hard work of the Basuto staff.

The wedding day itself was beautiful, the mountains round the valley and the little forest at its head were clear as crystal against the deep blue sky. Not for nothing was this part of Basutoland known as "the Switzerland of Southern Africa." By now the Howards had left and Tom Lawrence was the new District Commissioner. He was a lean and witty fellow, with an extremely jolly and rather scatterbrained wife Lucy, ten year old Sarah and the wiry little five year old twins Jane and Jenny.

I had hired the morning suit in Johannesburg, and assumed that as the jacket of the morning coat had fitted, the trousers would as well; this was not the case and they were significantly short in the leg. Even though this looked a bit odd, it didn't bother me at all as Uncle Bert and I walked towards the clamour of the crowd surrounding the little tin roofed church, nestling below the conifer wood. I was in another dream, of pure happiness this time. We climbed the stone steps and sat down in the coolness of the sandstone church. Suddenly the harmonium wheezed into life and a few seconds later Celia's white clad figure was alongside me and the wonderful old ceremony began.

The wedding

As Celia's father was ill and her mother had been unable to leave him, she was given away by my mother's brother, Uncle Bert, and my father's brother, Uncle Eric was my best man. The ceremony passed in a daze under Michael Hardy's eagle eye, his black beard bristling. A nuptial Mass followed, a hymn was sung by the Basuto choir, and rather to my surprise, Celia was unable to rise from her knees when it finally came to an end. "Get off my dress, if you don't mind," she muttered.

Blinking in the bright sun, we paused at the door, drinking in the smiling, multicoloured crowd, the trees, the mountains and the blue, blue sky. I sneaked a proper look at Celia and was stunned by her grace and beauty. She was followed by the three girls, Heather and Hazel Sidney and Foxy Lee, who was resplendent in her hastily made dress. The little procession made its way to somebody's big grey car, fluttering with white ribbons, and we drove the two hundred yards to the Maluti Inn where the ladies had prepared a great buffet in the conservatory.

Everybody was there, including Keith and Irene Whitelock who were prospecting for diamonds with a villainous looking crew of diggers. One of them, known as Black Pete, despite being white, had walked thirty-

31

five miles through the mountains from Mashai to be there and then he walked back again after it was all over.

Brian Lee, the local superintendent of police, had lent me his sword to cut the cake, and when the pieces had been passed round Heather, Hazel and Foxy fluttered around distributing food to the Basuto children sitting on the wall by the inn. After the meal there were speeches and photos, including one with the choir resplendent in their traditional grass hats and blankets. It all passed like a dream.

I had to do a round of the hospital when everyone had disappeared, but finally we were alone together. That night we were woken up by a tremendous crash on the tin roof. I leapt out of bed and cautiously ventured out onto the stoep. There was complete silence in the crystal moonlight; so, mystified, I returned to bed. Just as we were snuggling together again there was another tremendous crash, but this time one of the rose bushes in the garden was giggling. "You bastards!" I roared, shaking my fist into the darkness, and two or three dark figures, still giggling, stumbled off into the night.

Altogether an amazing day.

CHAPTER 3
THE SCHOOLMASTER

Basuto rondavels

"What on earth was that?" said Celia sitting bolt upright in the bed beside me. It was the morning after our first night in bed together. She had been woken by a muffled roar from the bathroom behind us.

"It's perfectly all right; it's only the chip heater. The convict fires it up every morning Relax. You may lie down again, " I said, coaxingly.

"Chip heater? What are you talking about? What do we want with chips at this hour of the day?" she demanded.

"The chips are the fuel, not the product," I reassured her, "You remember that tall cylinder in the bathroom I showed you?" She nodded. "Well, the convict stuffs chips of wood, twigs, anything he can find into the little door at the bottom, lights it, it roars up, and Bingo! Twenty gallons of hot water for the bath."

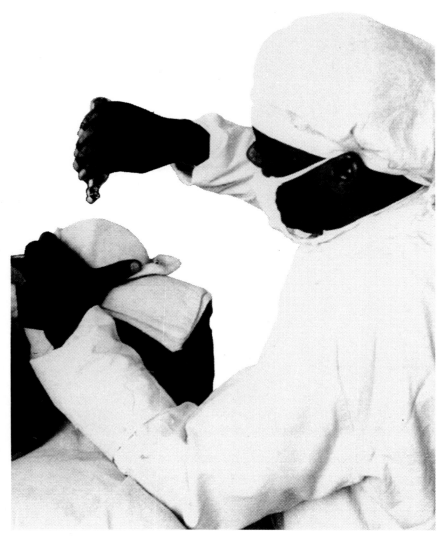

Butler Panyane gives a rag and bottle anaesthetic

Celia seemed satisfied and lay down again. "I'm not really happy about having convicts in the house," she said.

"Don't worry, everyone has one or two. The place would grind to a halt without them. Come on, let's laze around a bit. We don't have to get up for a few minutes."

Paying no attention, she slid the Basuto blanket off the bed, put it round her shoulders, walked to the window and stared out.

"It's beautiful here, quite beautiful. Just look at that mountain."

The massive bulk of Mount Sauer rose majestically against the blueness of the sky across the valley, directly opposite. A soft tablecloth of pink cloud was drifting lazily over its northern shoulder, lit by the rising sun. I clambered out of bed, put my arm round her shoulders and we watched, transfixed by the extraordinary spectacle.

The bath was enormous, with plenty of room for two. The water from the chip heater was blazing hot, but it was important only to put in enough cold water to make it just bearable, as there was no more hot water to come. Of the convict there was no sign, and the morning wallow developed over the coming days into a delightful ritual.

The three dogs, Larki, Topsy and Patachou, that Stephen and June Howard left behind with us when they were transferred to Maseru, were milling round as we sat down to our first breakfast together. They were full of character and gave us great delight.

Larki was a bull terrier who spent a great deal of time romancing various bitches round the camp and would return after a few days absence, bloody and exhausted. Near replicas of him were to be seen all over the place. Topsy was an ordinary terrier and a manic fetcher of thrown pebbles. She would stare at you with round, piercing black eyes, until you relented and threw the pebble yet again; this could go on for hours. Patachou was a black miniature French poodle, and completely unlike the stereotype. She was jolly and sporty, could run faster than the others and would dash towards me and leap into my arms with joy when I came home in the evenings or for lunch. These three were our companions for several months, and we were sorry to see them go when it was their turn to transfer to the capital.

When we had settled in and Celia had reduced the house to some kind of order, we let it be known that we wanted to learn something of the language, and one evening soon after, there was a knock at the door.

Standing outside was a small elderly man. He smiled. " How do you do? Kikine is my name. I used to be the village schoolmaster. I hear you would like to learn a little Sesuto."

We shook hands with him in turn. "Do come in Mister Kikine, would you like a cup of tea?" said Celia.

We sat enthralled as he gave us our first lesson in the history of the country and the rudiments of the language.

"*Sesuto* is the language we speak, *Lesuto* is *Sesuto* for *Basutoland*, the country of the Sesuto-speaking people. One Sesuto-speaking person is a *Mosuto*; more than one are *Basuto*. It is quite simple really," he explained.

"Our country was formed early in the last century when King Moshweshwe gathered the people on Thaba Bosiu, the Mountain of the Night. They had been scattered and driven up there by Chaka and his men; Chaka was the dreadful Zulu chief and warrior," he continued, "Thaba Bosiu is a flat-topped mountain where they could build a small town and be safe."

He was fascinating. His English was a bit old-fashioned as befits a schoolmaster, but perfect. He had an extraordinary aura of gracious kindliness. I felt a surge of affection for him.

"You will find that people will call you *Morena*. Literally translated it means 'Chief'', but it is used as a courtesy title. You are *Morena ngaka*, or chief doctor."

"We greet each other with the word *Dumela*, which means 'hello', followed by *Ntate* if you are addressing a man or '*Me* for a woman. More formally we say *Khotso!* which means 'peace', On special occasions, such as making a speech, we may say *Khotso! Pula! Nala!*, which means 'peace, rain and prosperity'. If someone is leaving you may say: *Tsamaia hantle*, which means 'go well' and to which the proper reply is *Sala hantle*, 'stay well'."

Mister Kikine came every week for several weeks, but in the end he decided that that was enough for the time being. We did not see him again for several months.

Meanwhile it was important to sort out the members of the hospital staff who had had me wished upon them. The core of the staff were a dispenser and three staff nurses.

Butler Panyane was my dispenser. He was just under medium height, lean and wiry, with a direct gaze and a quiet and careful mode of speech. He could give a rag and bottle anaesthetic, pull teeth, make up medicines and keep the double-entry ledger which showed the coming and going of goods, equipment and drugs. He was utterly reliable and a fine tennis player and I would have been lost without him. His wife, Claudia, was later promoted to sister-in charge of a hospital on the other side of the territory.

Butler was my interpreter and mentor. One day I was so upset by the number of patients who were making a terrific racket and crowding round the dispensary that I rushed out and shouted "*Voetsak!*". To my satisfaction they quieted down immediately and withdrew a few yards, but when I sat down again, Butler took me to task. "You never speak to people like that, doctor; that word is reserved for animals."

The three staff nurses were called Makhoa, Khaketla and Kalaka. They were always impeccable in their crisp white uniforms, maroon epaulettes and with a maroon band to their caps. Though there was no overt hierarchy, Florry Kalaka appeared to be in charge. She was small, round and compact, quiet and determined, with eyes that twinkled behind her glasses.

In addition to these four there were three midwives (who spent most of their time out and about in clinics and villages) five male and five female ward attendants, and two laundresses. I couldn't have asked for a better team.

There were three clinics which had to be served: Mashai, which was twenty minutes away by air over the mountains to the north, Sekake's, an hour or so by Land Rover to the west, and Sehlabatebe, two hours drive to the east, also by Land Rover.

The road to Sekake's follows the Orange River, which starts high in the Drakensberg, snakes its way west across Basutoland in a deep gorge, winds right across the Republic, and eventually pours into the South Atlantic ocean on the coast of what was then known as Southwest Africa,

The road to Sekake's

37

and is now called Namibia. Our road was really a sandy track which lay about two hundred feet above the river and followed its every curve. One fine day Butler and I were swerving and bouncing along this road in the Land Rover when we came across a taxi in distress. It was an ancient Chevrolet, full of women and children, animals and chickens, and the roof rack was piled high with their goods and chattels. Attached to the front of the roof rack was a pair of Kudu horns. It had come to rest at a point where a stream crossed the track, and was quite unable to mount the rise ahead.

"I put in plenty of petrol, *Morena,* but the engine stopped as we came down the hill, and now she won't go at all," said the taxi driver, tugging distractedley at his black beard, as we pulled up nearby.

I knew very little about cars, but it seemed that everyone else knew even less. I spent some time contemplating the engine, hoping for inspiration. After a while I clearly had to do something, so having diagnosed the copper pipe that went into the carburettor as the fuel line, I thought it would be a good idea to detach it from the carburettor and see if there was any petrol coming through. There wasn't.

"Try and start her now," I said, and the driver operated the electric starter, but no petrol came squirting out of the fuel pipe as the engine turned over.

After a bit more thought I noticed a wire going to the little pump in the fuel line, and concluded that it was electrically operated, and that it had packed up.

When I was a boy we had an ex-first world war naval pinnace with two huge Kelvin engines, and we used to bumble around the south coast of England in it. The fuel pump had failed and my father had had a gravity tank installed in a locker above the engine, which solved the problem. Could the same principle be applied here?

Looking around for inspiration, my gaze fell upon the Kudu horns on the roof rack. They seemed to be trying to tell me something. Suddenly the answer came to me.

"Butler, I wonder if we could do without one of those plastic bottles of medicine in the back?" He let down the tail gate, and I clambered in and rummaged amongst the bottles, picked one up and looked at the label. *Mistura pertussis.* There was no whooping cough about, so that could be replaced at a later date. I jumped out, emptied the polythene bottle into the ditch and with some difficulty managed to bend the copper fuel pipe up between the hood and the windscreen, and force the end through a hole dug in the cap of the bottle. The driver filled the bottle with petrol from his spare can, and together we managed to attach the cap and fuel pipe.

"Anyone got any string?" It was the work of a moment to lash the whole contraption to the Kudu horns, and to my relief the engine started this time, and away they went, cheering and waving.

I felt extremely pleased with myself as we drove on to take the clinic, which was surrounded by patients sitting patiently wrapped in their blankets. Fortunately it never crossed my mind that my action in saving the taxi was a gross misuse of government property.

* * *

When we arrived back at the hospital, Florry Kalaka appeared, wringing her hands. "It's Mister Kikine; he's terribly ill. I think he's dying."

The old schoolmaster looked awful. He tried to smile and speak, but all he could manage was a grimace of pain. His already frail body had withered away, but his abdomen was grossly distended. I percussed it gently all over, and found that it was full of both wind and fluid. I could only just feel his pulse which was fluttering along at a rate of about 130 beats to the minute. His blood pressure was too low to be sure about. Every now and then his eyes half closed, just revealing the whites.

It turned out that having been in reasonable health he had developed abdominal pain a week or so before, and he had gone downhill ever since. He was clearly dying and any operative procedure would probably accelerate the process. This poor old man, who had showed us such grace and loving-kindness was fading away before my eyes. Perhaps it would be kinder to let him go. Irresolute, I sent up a silent prayer.

When I had only been in Maseru a few days, David Standing, who had been operating under primitive conditions such as these for many years, said to me: *"If someone is dying of something in their abdomen there is no excuse for not having a look inside."* His words echoed in my head.

"If you can't do anything else, you can always stick in a drain and let it hang out." The words of a Surgical Registrar at Guy's when I was a student, and who went on to become a distinguished consultant.

At this point I did something that stood me in good stead when anxiety and fear were clouding my judgement; in my mind I turned myself into two people. I would pretend that I was a senior, experienced surgeon, who knew what to do, but didn't have to do it. Then I would pretend to be his Registrar and follow his orders. This mental trick separated the decision from the emotions that obscured it. The boss gave the orders but didn't have to follow them, and his Registrar had to follow them, but the decision wasn't his responsibility. What I had to do was quite clear.

"Take him to theatre" I said, "He'll need intravenous fluids, too. A litre of dextrose saline, to start with."

After I had put up the drip, I cleaned up his abdomen with

mercurochrome and gently inserted some 2% lignocaine to anaesthetise his stretched, parchment-like skin of the lower right side, using the finest needle we had. He was beyond flinching or responding in any way. Butler was seated at the head of the table, keeping track of the patient's carotid pulse and making sure that he could breathe as well as possible, though his breath was only coming in short, fitful gasps.

Florry handed me a scalpel and the tight skin parted at my first stroke. A few more strokes revealed the underlying muscle, such as it was, and the glistening peritoneal membrane which covered his intestines. I picked up a fold of the membrane, nicked it with the scalpel, and let it go.

It fell back into the wound, and suddenly a rush of brown, foul smelling fluid spurted out through the hole I had made. Several pints of this revolting pus poured out onto the concrete floor. When the flow had stopped I put in a corrugated rubber drain, cleaned and tidied him up, and taped a gauze dressing, backed with plenty of cotton wool, onto his now deflated abdomen. He seemed to have a lot of skin to spare.

"How is he?"

"Just the same, doctor; no worse," said Butler.

"Take him back to the ward, and give him a gram of Streptomycin daily and a million units of penicillin by injection four times a day, starting as soon as possible," I said. I did not think he had a chance of surviving.

He did not die. For some days it was touch and go, but thanks to careful and dedicated care from the three nurses he gradually recovered his strength, until at last he was well enough able to return to his home in the village adjacent to the camp.

"Many thanks, *Morena Ngaka*," he said as he gravely shook my hand when it was time to go. He turned and gathered himself together for as dignified an exit as he could manage. I stared after him for some time as he wobbled off on legs as thin as sticks.

* * *

Some days later a thick-set man with a black beard appeared at the door at the end of a long session seeing patients in the dispensary. He was holding a polythene medicine bottle with a hole in its cap.

"We all got home safely, and I thought you would like your bottle back, *Morena*," he said with a laugh.

I was telling Celia all about Mr Kikine and the taxi driver that evening, with my usual noisy gusto, when I noticed that her mind was not entirely with me, so I trailed off into silence. After a while she said:

"Something happened to me this morning."

I waited for more.

"I was walking back from the store when a man rushed up and grabbed my elbow saying *Come missis, come quickly.* He took me to his hut and there was a woman on the floor with a new-born baby. The cord and placenta were still attached. The mother seemed to be all right. At first I could not think what to do, but then I gathered the whole lot up in a blanket and carried it to the hospital with the man trotting beside me saying *Is there life? Is there life?"*

Totally untrained, in an alarming situation in a foreign land, she had kept cool and done the right thing. I was proud of her.

CHAPTER 4
A FATAL COUGH

Outpatient transport

She had huge dark almond eyes, and they seemed to be gazing somewhere far, far away. Her lovely round head with its tight black curls, her features so perfectly sculpted, her entire form so slim and relaxed .... she was indeed beautiful. I was seeing beauty everywhere now that I was married and released from self-imposed continence.

I had been at her bedside for a couple of hours now, plenty of time to think about these things. I adjusted the syringe taped into the crook of her elbow, and drew back a little blood to make sure it was still in the vein.

The TB ward was brand new when I arrived, its grey rendering contrasting sharply with the honey coloured stone of the rest of the hospital cut from the nearby quarry which provided the stone for most of the little town.

There were ten male and ten female beds, always full. Tuberculosis was rife; it was estimated that about one person in two hundred was affected. The disease probably came from milk in the first instance, as dealing with infected cattle demanded more resources and will than were available in Basutoland at that time. Then it would be passed on by coughing. Cattle couldn't just be slaughtered as a menace to health as they represented wealth, and played an essential part in the delicate rural economy, which already teetered on the brink of collapse, and which could not provide enough food to keep all the people free of malnutrition and even starvation.

So skinny cows grazed on the scanty grass, gave a pint or two of milk a day, and were even expected to pull things along when the need arose. Their dung was burned for fuel rather than returned to the sandy soil, which was then readily eroded by wind and rain. One of the senior nurses had recently returned to Maseru from a course in England. When asked for her impressions of the country she said that what struck her most was how fat and happy the cows were.

The young woman cleared her throat; was she going to cough again? From time to time she would be seized with a fit of coughing that brought a cup full of blood pouring from her lips. These fits could be aborted by immediate injection of morphine and it was the only way I could see to keep her from death. She was having intravenous fluids in her other arm, but if this state of affairs continued too long her blood would become so dilute that it could not sustain life. Indeed it was probable that she would die in any case. An artery in her lung had been eaten into by the TB and I had decided that everything else in the hospital would have to wait until she had been cough free long enough for a clot to form that was stable enough to stop the bleeding; and with luck the antibiotics would allow it to heal. There was no way of knowing whether it was the cough that caused the bleeding or the bleeding that caused the cough, but the morphine did seem to be stopping the bleeding for a while.

She had been quite well in herself until the day the tuberculosis ate through an artery in her lung and she suddenly brought up so much blood. Her family had had no idea that she was so ill.

Her pulse was weak and thready and blood pressure low; this was making her less likely to bleed, so I tried to keep the fluid replacement at a level that would not encourage her blood pressure to rise for the time being.

This was the third severe haemoptysis I had seen in the last few weeks. One of them had settled and gone home on therapy, but the other had died, which was infuriating as she had survived for three weeks without further bleeding, and I thought I had won.

It had happened like this. I had been exploring a dark corner at the back of the dispensary and came across a shelf of dusty old textbooks which had been there since the nineteen thirties. Thumbing through one of these fascinating old books, I had come across a chapter on tuberculosis. In the section on how to deal with people who bled severely from their lungs it said: *"Administer tincture of aconite until the pulse can no longer be felt."* Tincture of aconite? Surely that was a deadly poison, which affected the heart! Poison the heart until you can't feel the pulse? On the face of it a crazy thing to do.

Then I remembered a story current at Guy's when I was a houseman about somebody who was rushed into hospital after vomiting a lot of blood at a football match. The beleaguered young houseman had been unable to contact his superiors for advice, and decided off his own bat that the best thing was to lower the patient's blood pressure with appropriate therapy. This was completely contrary to the accepted teaching that the circulatory shock was dangerous, and it should be reversed by maintaining the blood pressure, until some method of stopping the bleeding, such as operation or giving freezing water through a tube, could be applied. The patient had survived, though the unfortunate houseman got into trouble for his unconventional therapy.

So maybe it wasn't such a stupid idea after all. Just because doctors were practising with limited resources in the nineteen thirties didn't mean that they were fools. Indeed Qacha's Nek in the sixties was probably quite like England in the thirties. But the problem was that we didn't even have tincture of aconite!

What I did have was a small supply of Ansolysen, a powerful drug for lowering blood pressure, so with some trepidation I gave the second woman a single twenty milligram tablet. The effect was almost instantaneous. Her blood pressure fell and she stopped bleeding. It rose again a bit after a while, but not enough. Three weeks later it still hadn't risen to 100 mm of mercury, and I felt that her kidneys might pack up if I didn't do something to bring her blood pressure back up again.

There was nothing in our very limited pharmacy designed to do this, but I thought that ephedrine, being an adrenaline-like substance, might have the desired effect.

Indeed it did. Over the next few hours her blood pressure rose to the proper level, about 120 mm of mercury, and a few hours after that she suddenly coughed up an enormous amount of blood, and died instantly. This was my first serious taste of how death could strike so suddenly and blow people away before my eyes, in this part of the world. It was so off-hand, that I couldn't really take it in.

So I was not worried about this particular young woman's low blood pressure, indeed, I hoped it would stay low. The most important thing was to try and stop her dreadful coughing.

Time passed. She slept awhile.

"Could you ring Celia and tell her I will be some time yet" I said when one of the nurses looked in. "Yes *Morena*, I will tell her," she replied.

It really should be possible to do something about all this TB, I thought. It was pretty hopeless starting people off on therapy and sending them home when you had no idea if they were carrying on with it. It was not possible to continue Streptomycin injections back in the village, which may be forty miles away in the mountains. One of the drugs you could take by mouth came in huge tablets, and six had to be taken four times a day, which is 720 a month. Coming back to the hospital for another bag of tablets often meant a major trek which they might not have the strength or opportunity to do.

There wasn't even a proper system of recording who was on treatment. Communications with the villages were effectively non-existent, so there was no way of recalling defaulters. Such records as did exist were often of little use because the names people were known by were liable to change as their situation and status changed.

Many people were weakened by malnutrition because they had nothing to eat except mealie porridge which contains no Vitamin B. This lack of vitamins eventually led to the peeling arms and tongue of pellagra, which were quite commonly seen in those who came to the dispensary,

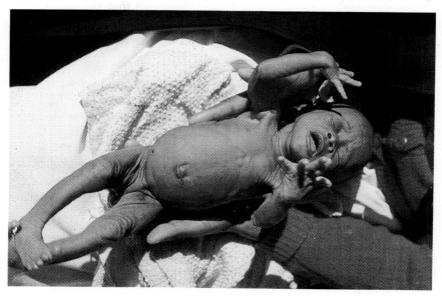

Starving baby

45

and if it was bad enough they became mentally disturbed as well. This malnutrition must make them vulnerable to any infective illness, TB included. So the few who made it to hospital were kept in on intensive treatment and proper food for about three months, in the hope that the tablets would clear up any infection that was left.

Tuberculosis could affect almost any organ of the body but it was commonest in the lungs. It caused problems with which we were ill equipped to deal. There was a man in the male ward next door one of whose lungs had collapsed with tuberculosis and his empty chest cavity had filled with fluid, so that he had difficulty breathing. I thought that I should try to drain this fluid off, so I had made an incision in his chest, pushed in the end of a rubber tube I had found in the store in Matatiele, probably meant for gas stoves, and fixed the other end of the tube under the water in a discarded transfusion bottle. The idea was that when the fluid had drained away, the negative pressure caused by the water rising in the tube would help the lung expand. It gave him a little relief but it hadn't made much difference to the collapsed lung. It had probably been like that for years, and was too shrunken and scarred ever to expand again.

Draining accumulations of fluid out of people seemed to occupy quite a lot of my time. For example someone, usually a man, would be admitted every week of two with a belly full of fluid, probably from cirrhosis or cancer of the liver. I had bought a splendid set of little perforated silver cannulae in Johannesburg, with a spike with a fat handle on the other end that you could slide inside any one of them. It was easy to push one through the skin after a small local anaesthetic and withdraw the spike. The only problem was finding a rubber tube small enough to attach, and stop the fluid spilling all over the place. I spotted a length of bicycle valve tubing in a trading store that turned out to be ideal for this purpose, though the tubes were too narrow to drain the 'anchovy sauce' pus (a description that intrigued medical students) from an amoebic liver abscess that had recently come in, and I had had to revert to my technique of stitching a length of rubber gas tubing so that one end rested in the abscess cavity, and the other drained into a bottle

The young woman seemed to be sleeping peacefully still.

I remembered learning about TB on the glassed-in balcony at Guy's, and how to the amazement of the students the Registrar had said "Tuberculosis is a killing disease, Miss Forstner, a killing disease!" in ringing tones whilst standing alongside the startled patient. How could anyone be so insensitive? Elizabeth Forstner was a fellow student.

I was a long way from Guy's now. I mused about the extraordinary chain of circumstances that had brought me to this place and was thinking about how Celia was creating such a lovely new home when suddenly the young woman sat bolt upright and was seized with a fit of violent coughing.

Blood was pouring from her mouth. I desperately tried to hang on to her arm so that I could inject some more morphine.

She fell back and lay still. I put my mouth over hers, held her nose and breathed into her bubbling lungs in an attempt to revive her. It was useless. She was dead.

When I was sure of this I left the ward. My eyes pricked with tears and I could taste her blood on my lips as I walked slowly back to the house.

I felt as if I had been wrestling with death, and death had won. The truth was that the whole business was pathetic: stupid and utterly futile.

I paused, looking in at the brightly lit window. I had a warm home and a future to look forward to. It suddenly came to me that I had not given a thought to the family of that poor young woman, or what they must be going through when they had so little in any case.

It may be fanciful to see it as a judgement on this insensitivity, but it was soon after that tragedy struck our own little world. Celia received a message from the District Commissioner that her father had died.

We wanted to be alone together for a while, so we drove away from the camp aimlessly and in silence until by chance we came across the two streams as they flowed across the track on the way to Tsoedike. We drew onto the verge and sat side by side for a long time in silence staring at the streams as they rippled and glittered in the sunlight. Celia had left her mother and father to join me at a time when he was seriously ill, and her mother had to look after him. Leaving them at such a time had been a wrench for Celia; it meant that she would not be able to help and support them and that neither of them would be able to come out for our wedding. Nevertheless, without hesitation they had encouraged her to join me, so far away.

And now her father had died, and she would never see him again, and he would never see the grandchild she was expecting.

We didn't say much; there was nothing much to say. Celia took things inwardly when she was distressed, and I knew how deeply she was shaken, and how she wished it could have been otherwise. He father had been ill in one way and another for years, but it was still a dreadful shock.

Even grief has to give way in the end, and we climbed back into the car and bounced back to the house in silence. I still had my round of the hospital to do.

47

CHAPTER 5
TRANSFIXION AND MAGGOTS

Cave paintings

"Hang on a minute, I think I've got it," I said. I was groping in this little boy's pus- filled ear with a safety pin which had been straightened out, and its point bent into a tiny hook. This crude device had proved to be marvellous for getting foreign bodies out of ears and noses. So long as I could see what I was doing, I could insert it past the object with the point aligned to the edge of the orifice concerned, then turn it until the hook was behind the object, and draw the foreign body out. One problem was keeping the boy still enough to do anything at all, and the other was seeing anything in the mess. I managed to swab out most of the pus with tiny pledgets of cotton wool in my smallest forceps, and at last what looked like the yellow skin of a maize seed appeared

Eventually I managed to draw the seed out and dropped it into a kidney dish. "Tell him he's a silly boy and not to do it again," I said to Florry. "What have we now?"

"The woman with the lip," she replied.

"Oh Lord, yes. That's going to be a problem. We should have kept this boy until last. As it is we'll have to disinfect the theatre now. Fortunately lips heal well."

The problem was that the woman had been in a fight with another woman over a man, and one of them had bitten a chunk out of the other one's lower lip. There was a huge piece of lip completely missing, about two-thirds of it, fortunately right in the middle.

For all their winning ways, the Basuto had a streak of violence that was liable to erupt at a moment's notice, or so it seemed. Only the previous week another woman had had the lobe of her ear bitten off, complete with her ear ring.

Because the wound was in her mouth, we couldn't use the usual mask and ether, so we had to numb her by injecting lignocaine and adrenaline into the substance of her lip, through the edges of the wound. Her eyes were covered with a towel so that she couldn't see what was going on, and Butler was murmuring into her ear to keep her calm.

I could still see the tooth marks, so I cut them away as best as I could, in order to reach uncrushed flesh and turn the "U" shaped wound into a "V". She bled a bit, but it was possible to staunch the blood by squeezing the edges of the wound until the bleeding stopped.

"Ordinary fine catgut please."

I sewed up the inside of her lip with separate stitches, and carried on out of her mouth and over the top, making sure that the lower edges of her lip were exactly in line. I finished off with four deep braided silk stitches between the lower edge of her lip and her chin to draw the muscle and flesh together. To my surprise and delight the whole thing came together beautifully, and though her new lower lip was only half as long as her upper lip, it didn't look at all bad.

The next operation was the removal of a large ganglion, or swelling from a tendon sheath, on the back of a woman's right hand. She had come to the dispensary the day before. It was obviously a ganglion, because it lit up like a red lantern when I pressed my torch against it.

"These things are supposed to go away if you whack them with the family Bible," I said to Butler. "I've never tried it on one this big, though. Ask her to lay her hand on the desk, and hang onto her wrist."

I fetched one of the heavy, ancient textbooks from the shelf, blew off the dust, and holding it in both hands, brought it down smartly on the back of her hand. This had no effect on the swelling, so I tried it again. I remembered how a local healer in Leribe had demonstrated his technique for a ganglion. Before I could say anything he had produced a rusty safety pin, thrust it into the swelling and given it a good wiggle. This method was a bit too crude for even my surgical skills, so instead I gave her hand a final thump, but the ganglion just stayed there as large as ever.

"I'm afraid I am going to have to excise it. Could you arrange for her to be put on the list tomorrow, please Butler?" I said.

So here she was, with her lower arm carefully wrapped in a sterile towel. I stood by, masked and gowned holding a gauze swab in a pair of long locking forceps, while Butler put her to sleep. I dipped the swab in a gallipot of iodine.

"Unwrap her arm please, nurse."

I stepped forward with my swab. Her arm had been beautifully cleaned and prepared, but of the ganglion there was no sign.

"Show me her other hand." Still no ganglion.

"Are we sure this is the right woman?"

"Yes, doctor, it is certainly the right woman," said Butler, "It is the one you hit with the book yesterday."

"Ah well. Yes indeed. You had better bring her round, then. The book seems to have done the trick." I felt a bit foolish, and wondered whether to complain that somebody should have told me that the ganglion had disappeared, rather than prepare a normal hand, but thought better of it. I looked silly enough already.

After a few more minor operations, I strolled back to the house for lunch. Celia, who was already showing a bit of a bulge from her developing pregnancy, was chatting to her paint-daubed sister Belinda, who had come to stay for a few weeks.

Belinda was studying at the Slade school of art, and was highly imaginative, perceptive and rather unpredictable. In fact she had an artist's temperament. The sisters were extremely fond of each other, and had been painting a mural of a Basuto village in the new children's ward. They had just completed a silhouette of a little boy, to which I had added a toy lorry made out of wire and tin lids, in the foreground. The picture was coming on well; later they would let me put in some shadows, which I felt brought the whole thing to life, and with which I was inordinately pleased. Painting the shadow of a passing chicken, I had found to be particularly taxing.

Once Belinda had recovered from an infected heel picked up wandering round Rome, we were able to show her around. She was enchanted with all she saw, and was particularly pleased with the Bushman cave paintings that were to be found under many of the overhanging sandstone outcrops round about. These were painted in varying shades of ochre and most of them depicted men with barbed spears hunting buck. We came across one extraordinary figure that looked for all the world like a crusader in chain mail and surcoat. The best way to see these paintings was to fill your mouth with water and spray it all over them, so that they stood out against the dusty yellow rock in all their glory. I doubt if conservators would agree with this particular method, but it was common practice then.

After lunch one day soon after Belinda had arrived, I strolled down to the mortuary, where the corpse of an old lady was awaiting my skills as a forensic pathologist. A ward attendant had lit a little cone of incense to mask the smell, and the instruments were laid out, ready.

"They say she was killed with a spear, *Morena*," he said.

When I was at Guy's as a houseman, I had asked the Pathologist if he would teach me how to do a post-mortem .

"Waste of time, my boy," he had replied, "You'll never have to do one." That was the end of the matter.

Now it was rare for a month to go by without some corpse being found. As District Medical Officer it fell to me to conduct the post-mortems, with the District Commissioner acting as magistrate and coroner.

This old lady had a small wound just to the left of her breast bone, so I cut out her sternum and opened out her ribs. I found that I could easily push my finger through the spear hole into her chest cavity. Below that I could see her pericardium, the membrane which covers the heart, which also had a slit in it, so presumably her heart had been pierced, and that would have caused her death. However when I cut open her heart I found that the hole passed in through the front and out through the back, entering her lung. Hauling her lungs out of the way I could see the wound still carried on, penetrating the back of her chest wall.

"Hang on a bit; let's turn her over," I said, and together we gave her a heave onto her side. Sure enough there was an exit wound in her back. "My God, she's been completely transfixed." I said incredulously, "That must have been a hell of a thrust."

I prepared my report and read it out at the inquest. The court room was full and the proceedings lengthly as everything had to be translated from English into Sesuto and back again. A spear made of a twisted rod of mild steel was produced. So that was the weapon!

"How rapidly would you estimate death to have occurred?" asked Tom Lawrence, District Commissioner and presiding magistrate.

"I would have expected death to have been instantaneous," I replied, "it was a terrible wound."

"Thank you, doctor, you may stand down."

Later I happened to meet Tom outside his office. "About your report at the inquest. You said that you would have expected death to have been instantaneous," he said, "Well, there is good evidence that she ran round her hut several times before collapsing."

Amazing. Yet another example of the extraordinary toughness of the Basuto. No wonder they were particularly sought after as shaft-sinkers, who were a sort of foreman, in the gold mines of the Rand.

A few weeks later, another victim of violence came into the hospital. Heaven knows what misdemeanour he had committed, but the punishment was savage. He had had his left leg systematically smashed with an iron bar, so that his tibia was broken in several places. His lower leg was just a wobbly piece of meat with a series of chunks of bone in it. It must have been horribly painful when they did it, but he was quite calm, glad perhaps that the painful bit was over, and that all he had to do now was to get better.

I was concerned that such a ghastly injury would go septic and never heal. Or that he would develop osteo-myelitis, and maybe die of septicaemia. But he clearly saw his recovery as my problem, and he wasn't going to waste his energy worrying about it.

I could do no more than clean him up, lay his leg out as straight as possible, prop his foot up at the correct angle, dress it with sterile gauze and cotton wool and cover the whole mess with a thick layer of home made plaster of Paris bandage and hope for the best. Maybe Penicillin, Streptomycin and some decent food would do the rest.

When we finally removed the plaster from the man's leg a couple of months later it was crawling with maggots, and the stench was appalling, but the wound was clean and healing beautifully. The maggots only liked rotten meat, and they had done a marvellous job of tidying things up.

My confidence, which fluctuated wildly with the flow of events, was beginning to return, so it was inevitable that two disasters should come my way.

The first disaster was the simpler. A man dropped down apparently dead just outside the hospital gate, and I rushed out to apply external cardiac massage and mouth-to-mouth artificial respiration, with absolutely no success whatsoever.

The second was much more alarming. A middle aged man was brought in *in extremis* wracked with terrific gasping breaths. He was in a terrible state, straining and heaving in a tremendous effort to fill his lungs. Thinking this must be some kind of asthma I laid my stethoscope on his chest and found to my surprise that air was rushing in and out of it without impediment.

It is difficult to think straight in the presence of such distress, but I had to try and come up with something, because clearly he couldn't keep this up much longer.

I had read that something a bit like this occurs when there is too much acid in the blood and the kidneys can't get rid of it, so the body tries to solve the problem by blowing off large quantities of carbon dioxide, but I had never come across it.

The only thing I could think of that should in principle give him some relief, and perhaps enable him to survive long enough to be flown to specialists in Durban or Bloemfontein, was to perform a tracheotomy. This should reduce the amount of air that was being re-breathed at each gasp, so that the carbon dioxide would be more quickly dispersed. There was a silver tracheotomy set in the theatre cabinet, so I asked Florry to boil it up while I studied my beloved Hamilton Bailey's *Emergency Surgery*.

There was no question of giving him a general anaesthetic, so I froze the front of his throat, just below his larynx, with an injection of Lignocaine and adrenaline, which was difficult because he couldn't keep still. I made a vertical incision and exposed the first four rings of his trachea, and holding the scalpel like a pen and resting my hand on his breast bone, as advised by Hamilton Bailey, thrust the scalpel firmly but carefully through the second, third and fourth rings. He gave a terrific cough, spattering us all with blood. After the fit was over, I clipped the corners off the rings to make a hole through which his breath came whistling, and Florry passed me a curved tracheotomy tube. I slipped it in through the hole and removed the articulated introducer, the blunt point of which projected from the end of the tube, and held it there while Florry organised the dressings, and taped it round his neck to hold it in position.

I wish, I wish, I wish that this could have saved him, but it didn't. He was only slightly relieved and he died a couple of hours later.

CHAPTER 6
HISTORY AND A STABBING

DC in full fig

Saturday afternoon tea at the tennis club hut just outside the camp was a delightful ritual. I cannot remember anyone actually playing tennis, but the expatriate community gathered for a weekly gossip while nibbling sandwiches carefully prepared by the ladies of the camp. I was no good at gossip so I would engage in mock mortal combat with the two splendid little Petersen boys who would bash me up, hurl me to the ground and jump up and down on me in triumph.

If there was no such fun in the offing I would read from one of the old books in the library at the back of the hut. I was particularly intrigued with a book called *The Campaign of the Cataracts*, about Kitchener's ultimately unsuccessful attempt to rescue General Gordon from Muhammed Ahmad al-Mahdi's siege of Khartoum. The navy had built special boats that were hauled up the cataracts of the Nile with ropes, while the army advanced on either side of the river. It was a stupendous effort, even if it arrived too late. A heroic failure. I laid the book aside and considered the wonder of the British Empire in its heyday. When I was a boy we were proud that a huge chunk of the world on our little tin globe was coloured red, but the whole massive enterprise had disintegrated like dew before the morning sun since the war, and little Basutoland was one of the last outposts left. It never crossed my mind to doubt the legitimacy of our Empire. This was how things were, and I was anxious to do my bit while there was still a job to be done. As Basutoland had asked to join the Empire in the first place, that was legitimacy enough. In a few more years they would be independent anyway.

We certainly still observed Imperial protocol at Qacha's Nek. At the last Queen's Birthday Parade Tom Lawrence had dressed up in his white tropical suit, solar topee and sword, and saluted the Union Jack to the sound of a bugle. The only snag was that no policemen were available to form a guard of honour as they were all out on patrol, so the prisoners were marched down from the gaol to take their place. Very smart they were with their red Tam o' Shanters, red and white striped jerseys, long khaki shorts and sandals. They obviously enjoyed the outing.

"You don't seriously believe that the British have held on to Basutoland because of what we can get out of it?" I had asked Butler Panyane one day as we were bouncing along in the Land Rover to the clinic at Sehlabathebe. My impression was that good old Britain was protecting and supporting this little country more out of charity than in the hope of gain. Not very generously admittedly, for example the drugs and dressings bill for a million people for the previous year had been only £50,000, but half a loaf is better than no loaf at all.

I was astonished when I found out how little Britain was putting in to the territory, but maybe this was not so surprising when there was no apparent return for the investment. "I would rather not talk about it," he replied.

"Come on, Butler, tell me what's on your mind."

"I would rather not, as I have been in trouble for my opinions in the past. Things are not as they seem."

He was not to be drawn any further, so I did not press him at the time. I snapped the *Campaign of the Cataracts* shut and tried to think the matter through. What could Butler have meant? I had heard that several thousand Basuto soldiers had been drowned when their ship was torpedoed in the war, so they certainly had earned our gratitude, but surely there was nothing to gain from this beautiful but barren little country; there were no serious resources that could be exploited. British shareholders might have earned a few bob from the Oxbow Lake scheme high in the mountains if it had ever come to fruition. This was a huge hydro-electric scheme which would have involved damming back the Orange River near its source. It would have provided power and water to the Republic, but the South African government would have none of it. They didn't want to be at the mercy of little Basutoland who would have been able turn the switch on and off at will, so there was no investment and the scheme had failed.

What else had the country to offer? There was no surplus produce; maize had to be imported just to keep the people fed, so there was no profit there. Diamonds? Small numbers of stones were being found, but the output was pathetic compared with that of the mighty diamond fields of Southwest Africa.

What about gold?

Maybe that's what Butler meant. Black gold; the mine workers themselves; slavery brought up to date.

What if Basutoland had to be kept half starved but calm, to supply recruits for the gold mines of the Rand? The miners would be grateful for the peanuts they were paid, and their work would continue to line the pockets of British shareholders. I dismissed the idea at once; we were here to serve, not to exploit anybody. Our Government would never sink so low as to connive at such things. If that was what Butler thought he was clearly deluded.

Such musings were cut short by the time we were back home. Florry was on the phone. "A young woman has just been brought in, doctor, she has been stabbed in the abdomen and she isn't very well."

The young woman was indeed sad and subdued in her calico night gown. She had an incision about an inch and a half long just to the right of the midline, about three inches above her pubic symphysis, but her pulse rate was barely raised and her blood pressure normal. There was no blood to be seen. I tapped the middle finger of my left hand with the same finger of my right hand resting on her flank, to see if there was any extra dullness there which would indicate an accumulation of fluid inside her abdomen. Then we rolled her onto her right side to see if any dullness disappeared, as it would if fluid had drained to her left side and her guts floated to the top. I couldn't detect any change in resonance.

"I'll put up an intravenous drip and just watch her for now. Give her a hundredth of a grain of Atropine by injection in case we have to operate. Temperature, pulse and blood pressure to be charted every quarter of an hour. Is the theatre ready?" I said.

"Everything is ready, doctor. We thought you might need it," said Florry.

"We'll give her an hour," I said.

After putting up the drip I walked back to the house for a cup of tea, and Johnny Toolan, one of Keith Whitelock's gang of diamond prospectors, was there, talking to Celia. Johnny was very popular, especially with women, for he had a lively personality and loads of Irish charm. He was liable to burst into song too, and had a fine resonant baritone.

> *I was down by the glen side*
> *When I met an old woman;*
> *She was pickin' young nettles*
> *And she ne'er saw me comin'.*
> *So I listened awhile*
> *To the tune she was hummin':*

> *Glory-oh, Glory-oh*
> *To the bold Fenian men.*

Sinn Fein and the IRA were ancient history at that time, suitable only for such sentimental songs, and we all joined in the chorus. It would be some time before the Troubles in Northern Ireland broke out again.

After half an hour I couldn't stand the waiting any longer, so I phoned the hospital and was told that the young woman's pulse was rising steadily and her blood pressure was beginning to fall.

"Call Butler, would you, Florry? I'll be down in five minutes." I hung up. "This might interest you, Johnny, would you care to watch?" He walked down to the hospital with me. I gave him a mask and asked him to keep well out of the way.

Butler soon had the patient asleep, and dripped a little ether onto the mask from time to time to keep her under. I was standing by her right side and little Florry was standing on a box opposite me with the tray of instruments to hand.

I made a left paramedian incision, and as I opened her peritoneal cavity it became apparent that there was a good deal of blood in there.

The United Nations had recently given us a foot operated suction machine, and I lifted her guts to one side and then the other, pumping with my foot to suck the blood out as I went, and finally swabbed her insides dry. I waited to see if more blood would appear, but it didn't. It must have come from somewhere, and I couldn't possibly sew her up again without finding where it was coming from, as she would die if the bleeding didn't stop.

Florry was holding her abdomen open with retractors, which was difficult as she had to pull against the muscles. Too much ether can be fatal, so it would have been dangerous to give the patient enough to make sure that her muscles were completely relaxed.

"I'm sorry, doctor, but I can't hold her open much longer," said Florry. That would be a problem as I still couldn't find the source of the bleeding. I could feel the whisper of panic beginning to rise somewhere deep inside me. Johnny was standing by, arms folded.

"Johnny, would you scrub up? Florry can't hold out much longer, and we can't stop here.

"Sure," said Johnny cheerfully, "Happy to give it a go. How do you do it?"

By now Florry was trembling with the effort of trying to keep the incision open. "You can let her go, now Florry, " I said as I straightened my aching back and neck and clasped my hands as a nurse instructed Johnny on the intricacies of scrubbing, gowning and gloving up.

Johnny made an excellent retractor and I was able to inspect the young woman's intestines minutely; but I could find no source of bleeding on the guts themselves, in the omentum that attached them to her posterior abdominal wall, or anywhere else inside her abdomen. In my desperation I repeated the inspection several times to no avail. This had taken well over an hour so far and we had got nowhere. I would simply have to close her up soon or the operation would finish what the stabbing had started.

I took another look at the stab wound, inside and out, and spotted something I had been too preoccupied to notice before; there was a swollen blood clot in the wound itself, within the substance of her abdominal wall. A gleam of hope lifted my spirits. The inferior epigastric artery! Maybe the knife had severed the artery that runs up the lower part of the front of her abdomen on that side, and the blood had been pouring into her abdomen from there, rather than from some other internal wound. I cleared the clot and closed the stab wound in her abdominal wall from the inside with deep, strong catgut stitches. I had a final look around. There was no sign of any further bleeding. "OK, that's it. I'm going to close her up now," I said, "You can take those retractors out now, Johnny".

58

Closing her abdomen was easier said than done as she seemed to have far too many guts for the available space, and as fast as I tucked them in at one end they popped out at the other. It was like trying to bury balloons in a bath full of water. Eventually, by gradually sewing down from the top and tucking them in as I went, they had all gone back, and sewing up the remaining layers didn't take long. By the time I had finished, Johnny was cutting the ends of the stitches as I held them up for him, with surprising precision.

"Will she be all right?" said Johnny later that evening as we sat around with a can of Castle Lager each, while the adrenaline seeped out of my system and I began to calm down. Celia had sensibly gone to bed.

"Good question. Can't say, really. She stood the operation quite well, but I expect tugging her guts about like that will lead to paralytic ileus, so we will have to suck and drip her for a few days. If she gets over that her chances are pretty good."

"What's paralytic ileus?"

"If you maul the guts about like that they become paralysed for some stupid reason, and then they simply inflate with wind, moving nothing on, and the patient can die of vomiting."

"I'll send one up for her. I may never go to Mass, but I'm still a good Catholic."

"You do that. She needs all the help she can get."

Johnny's prayer seemed to do the trick. There was an anxious couple of days before I heard the first tinkle of bowel sound in her inflated abdomen, and it was a great relief to us all when she finally passed wind and her tummy began to shrink.

I think that her first fart gave me almost as much relief as it gave her.

Her skin stitches were removed a week later, and her wound healed well. A few more days to recuperate and she was off home to her village clutching a bag of Ferrous sulphate tablets to help replace the blood she had lost, wobbling, but at least alive.

That was one of my good days.

CHAPTER 7
HUBRIS AND NEMESIS

On the road to Sehlabathebe

"Here, Celia: Hamilton Bailey tells you how to do a Symes'
amputation" I said one day as we were eating breakfast on the *stoep*. The
sun was shining, the air as clear as crystal apart from the sweet-smelling
smoke lazing up from the chimneys across the way. Hamilton Bailey's
great text book, *Emergency Surgery*, was open beside me on the table.

"What's a Symes' amputation?" asked Celia.

"It's a cunning way of removing someone's foot, but leaving them something half-way decent to walk with. Here, have a look." I passed the book across and pointed to the diagram.

"Wow! Would you really be able to do that?" said she, sceptically.

"I don't know - I've never tried, but I think so; it doesn't look very difficult. There's a woman in the ward with a horrible black, fungating growth the size of a small cauliflower growing out of the ball of her foot, and it is stopping her walking. With a Symes' amputation we could remove the tumour, and the foot isn't any use to her anyway. The really cunning thing is that you can saw the knobs off the bottom of the leg bone, remove the heel bone and then fold the heel under, which gives you a splendidly tough stump to walk on, even if it's a bit short."

I took the book back and read and re-read the text until it was imprinted on my mind. I had cut off a leg in the past under supervision, and it was relatively easy. I had also had six weeks orthopaedic experience as a house officer in England and was quite used to bones and joints. All in all, I felt I could do it.

And so it proved. Butler Panyane put the patient to sleep with his usual skill with the dropping bottle of ether and I applied a tourniquet to the leg. I inked in the incision line on the skin in such a way that there would be enough skin to be able to close the wound when the foot had been removed. When I was happy with the line, I cut along it, exposing the front of the ankle joint. Carefully tying off the arteries as I went, I cut the ligaments in front of the ankle with a strong bladed scalpel and removed the bones of the foot. The operation went smoothly and I dropped the horrible foot with its tumour into the bin. I folded the heel flap up under the end of the woman's stump, put in a couple of rubber drains and sewed it up. *If there are any 'dog ears' at the points where the original incisions met, these should be removed with scissors* said Hamilton Bailey. There were, so I snipped them off.

The only serious problem was that it had proved impossible to clean the tumour completely and the whole thing went septic, as Hamilton Bailey had warned, but the rubber drains let out the pus, and with the aid of penicillin, streptomycin and sulphonamides it all settled down and in due course she was sent home to her village with a useable stump. As she never came back, it was reasonable to assume that she would continue to improve. The growth was presumably cancerous, perhaps a melanoma, though in that case it was surprising that it had grown so large without spreading elsewhere. So her outlook was far from good, but she should have been more comfortable, and with luck would be able to walk again.

As this seemed to have worked reasonably well, I began to feel increasing confidence in my surgical skill. Life was looking good and a wonderful weekend was to follow.

There was a pool with a rocky ledge beside it, in the Sejabatho river, just a few miles out of camp along the dirt road to Sekake's, reached by a scramble down the valley. So Celia made a picnic, various children were gathered together from the camp, we bumped and slithered down to the pool, and a session of impromptu water sports began. A particular favourite, gleaned from my youth, was *Sink the Bismarck!* in which you had to stand on the ledge with one finger under your nose (Hitler's moustache), and your right arm stiffly raised, shout "Heil Hitler", jump in holding your nose with your other hand, and stay under water as long as possible. Ivan Petersen particularly enjoyed watching his boys do this, as he had been a Hurricane pilot busting Rommel's tanks in North Africa during the war, though he declined to take part in the game itself.

Lounging in the sun, full of food and happiness, I said to Celia "You know, women often come along with fibroids in their uterus wanting them dealt with. I remember someone telling me that if you put a tourniquet round the uterus, say a rubber catheter, you can pop the fibroids out. I think I'll have a go next time a suitable patient turns up".

And it did prove both easy and successful. The fibroids popped out like ping-pong balls of various sizes, and big bold catgut stitches with a curved needle gathered the cavities in the uterus together, so that they didn't bleed when the tourniquet was released. The operation was reasonably quick as well; it was important not to take long, because even with a prior injection of atropine, people's chests began to bubble after an hour or so inhaling raw ether from a face mask.

I was beginning to feel so much more confident about my surgical skills that I yearned to take on something more difficult, so I rang Jack Smith, a GP in Matatiele 35 miles away down in the Republic, who did a lot of operating, and asked if I could assist at a hysterectomy some time, which he was happy to agree to.

Jack was a skilled operator, and worked with great speed. He opened the abdomen, grasped the uterus with toothed forceps, and at his request I drew it to one side. Jack then placed two clamps between the ovary and the uterus and snipped carefully down between them with long handled scissors until he reached the top of the vagina. He tied off the tissue held in the clamps and then repeated the procedure on the other side.

"You have to be careful to avoid the ureters (the tubes which carry the urine from the kidneys to the bladder) as they run close by here, and you are really in trouble if you cut them. The ovarian and uterine arteries should be held in the clamps, but if you damage the ureter there is hell to pay. It's difficult to see, too."

Then he cut out the uterus with its fibroids, leaving the stump of the cervix behind, oversewed the stump with catgut to stop the bleeding,

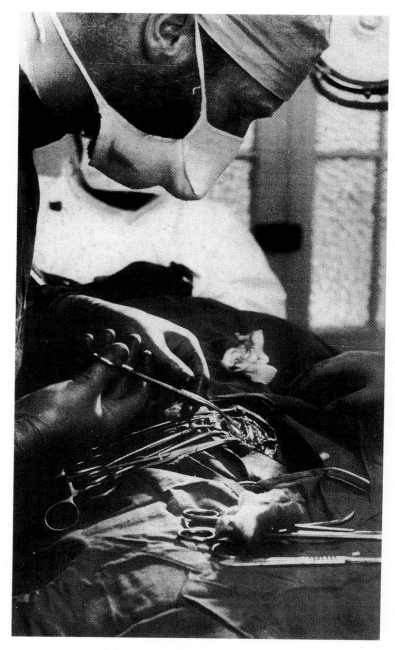

Bush surgery

checked for any bleeding points that needed tying off, and sewed up the abdomen. It was so simple and straightforward; all over in little more than twenty minutes.

After a most elegant afternoon tea with the Smiths, as we were rattling and banging back up the escarpment to Qacha's Nek, I was already planning in my head how to apply my new found knowledge.

The chance came a couple of weeks later. A woman in her late fifties with abdominal discomfort and heavy periods from her extensive fibroids wanted them removed. They can recur if you pop them out, it would be much better to do a hysterectomy. The operating theatre was set up, instruments prepared, patient put on the table; Butler dropped ether onto the mask until she was well asleep and the operation began.

The operation went well enough, but it took far longer than intended because I was so scared of cutting the ureters. I took tiny snips with the long scissors down the side of the uterus in case a ureter was concealed in the tissue.

"Her pulse is weak, doctor," said Butler. Her breathing was bubbly and it dawned on me that she might be running into serious trouble. Despite this there was no turning back and I had to finish the procedure. Thinking that the operation would only take half an hour or so I hadn't even put up an intravenous drip, and there was no one else who could put one up for me during the operation. I put one up afterwards, but it was too late; the patient never came round from the anaesthetic. She had died.

I was appalled. Through my own stupidity and utter failure to realise my lack of skill I had killed someone. I, a doctor who was supposed to make people better, had killed someone, or at least someone had died as a result of my crass overestimate of my surgical skill. Precisely why she died was not clear, though the long time she was under ether must have had something to do with it. The awful thing was that the operation was neither urgent nor essential; fibroids may be uncomfortable, but as a rule they are not otherwise immediately dangerous. I felt beyond forgiveness.

When I broke the news to the relatives, they responded by expressing their gratitude for all I had done with the usual Basuto grace, which made me feel even worse.

In despair I felt I had to tell the District Commissioner immediately, so I went round to his office as soon as I could get away

"Tom, I had to come and see you...... I have just killed a patient..... Her operation was not essential and I thought I could do it..... But I couldn't...... She's died, and as District Commissioner and magistrate I'm telling you about it...... It was completely my fault....."

"Hang on a bit, calm down and tell me what happened." So I did.

Tom Lawrence pondered for a while. "What did the relatives say?"
"That's what's so awful. They thanked me for trying!"

"Are you going to do a post mortem?"

"Yes, of course, if the relatives agree."

"Bring me the report when you have done it."

So I re-opened the wound and inspected the operation site. It was fine. The ureters were intact and there was hardly a teaspoonful of blood in the pelvic cavity. Nothing had gone wrong with the operation itself. I took the report to the DC.

"So nothing awful happened in the operation, and the relatives have made no complaint". He pondered awhile. "You have no way of knowing what else might have been wrong with the patient. Death is never very far away in Africa: we often don't know quite why. Off you go and get on with your work."

"But........"

"Off you go!"

*　*　*

That wasn't the only blow to my morale. Our Elsie had a beautiful teenage daughter on whom she had poured all her love and hopes. She was a strapping young woman, always cheerful, and proud of her impeccable school uniform. She was admitted to the hospital *in extremis* with what appeared to be typhoid fever, and in a few hours she was dead. Apart from putting up a drip and giving her chloromycetin, I did nothing.

As the ululating procession passed by at the funeral, I remembered David Standing's advice again: *"If someone is dying of something in their abdomen, there is no excuse for not having a look inside."* It had worked for Mr Kikine.

It just might not have been typhoid. With no laboratory facilities it was impossible to be sure what it was. She had not had much diarrhoea, and it might have been something else in her abdomen mimicking the typhoid that was around. I should have operated on her even if there was a risk of killing her. She would die in any case if I did nothing. I should have opened her abdomen in case there was something that could be done, but because of my recent experience I didn't dare.

The lack of diagnostic facilities was beginning to wear me down. Half the time I had no idea what was going on. While I could keep my head if there was only one desperately ill patient in the hospital at the same time, I found it extremely difficult to think clearly if there were two or three. I felt drained. Perhaps it would be best if I resigned before I did any more damage.

Some time later, bouncing along in the Land Rover to hold a clinic at Sehlabathebe, I hit a pothole. Butler rose from the passenger seat and struck his head smartly on the roof of the Land Rover.

"Sorry Butler, but I can't seem to concentrate. I can't help thinking about that poor woman and Elsie's daughter. I shouldn't be here in Basutoland. I should go somewhere and get properly trained. The Basuto don't deserve an incompetent like me. Why are they so forgiving?"

"Basuto people have a different way of looking at death." said Butler.

I pulled the Land Rover over to the side of the track and put on the brake and switched off the engine. "What did you say?"

"To Basuto people when someone dies they don't go away. They simply step sideways into another place that is still going on. They are always with you; you just can't see them, that's all."

I started up the Land Rover and pulled away. I had much to think about. I felt a bit better. Maybe I would see my time through after all.

CHAPTER 8
A POTENT SMELL AND AN OLD MUSKET

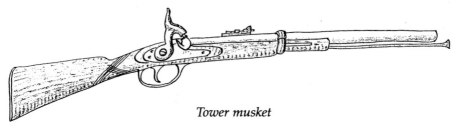

Tower musket

It was still snowing heavily, but when the weather cleared the mountains reared up like white ghosts round the valley as I, well prepared with porridge, toast, marmalade and coffee walked briskly down the drive and round the corner to the little hospital. It was bitterly cold. As usual the wards were full but Florry Kalaka assured me that all was well and no-one had deteriorated during the night.

The ward round would come later, but first there would be people who had walked or ridden in to be seen. I crunched across the track to the dispensary, its red tin roof obscured by an icing of snow; a plume of smoke pouring from the metal chimney. There was a small huddle of blanketed figures waiting on the stoep. Inside the dark consulting room, Butler had managed to create a cosy atmosphere, with the help of the glowing stove in the corner. "Good morning, doctor," he said with a smile, "there are only a few people to see, so we shouldn't be very long." He opened the door and called in the first patient.

Outpatients usually followed a pattern. Most patients were women, probably because most men were away working in the gold mines of Johannesburg. As there were no facilities for testing anything, diagnosis was reduced to informed guesswork, though it was usually possible to distinguish between serious and not so serious problems.

One common complaint was *kaofela*. This was Sesuto for "everywhere". The patient would say that they had pain everywhere, and when asked how long they had had it, would reply "Since I was

67

born". No other information was forthcoming and as I could not find anything wrong after a brief examination, Butler would give them an injection of Vitamin B. We took the view that as practically everyone was short of vitamin B and quite a few had the peeling tongue and scaling arms of overt pellagra, an injection would do them good. Injections were very popular as being the strongest kind of medicine.

Others would complain of abdominal pain and a discharge down below. If pressure in the lower abdomen produced a grimace of pain, this was considered to be gonorrhoea and Butler gave an injection of long acting penicillin. There were coughs, colds and bowel upsets for which Butler made up bottles of appropriate medicine from the shelves of Winchesters in the back room. Everyone had to pay two shillings, whether they only received a bottle of medicine or whether their case was such that they had to be admitted to hospital.

When the last patient had been seen, I walked back through the snow with Butler, past the hitching rail with one sad snow-dusted mule attached, up the steps to the hospital and a cup of coffee in the staff nurses' tiny office.

We had scarcely settled when there was a commotion outside. A raggedy bundle was being carried in from the stoep to the ward by some men, their Basuto hats and blankets all snowy. A few minutes later Florry appeared: "We've just admitted a woman who says she has been shot by her boyfriend. She is quite well and ready for you to see."

So many extraordinary things seemed to happen in Qacha's Nek that I was beyond being perturbed by this startling news. I followed Florry into the female ward where a dozen women were lying in their iron-framed beds. I mentally blessed the Public Works men who had recently replaced the mud and dung on the walls with plaster. It would be easier to keep the place clean. Dung is reputed to be full of tetanus bugs, yet oddly no-one seemed to get tetanus. Even though septic, clean and maternity cases had previously all been nursed in the same dung-plastered ward, sepsis did not seem to spread. Maybe the bad bugs couldn't get a look-in because of the large numbers of good bugs in competition with them.

The woman was perhaps forty years old, dressed in a white calico gown and with her head scarf still in place. Her left arm was exposed, with a dressing on her shoulder. When this was removed it showed a hole the best part of an inch across in the side of the deltoid muscle. "Can you lift your arm?" "*Uh uh*" she replied, shaking her head. I turned to the nurse. "So what happened?"

There was a brisk exchange in Sesuto between the patient and Florry Kalaka.

Ox wagon in the snow

"She says that she was sleeping in her hut on the mountainside, and in the middle of the night her boy friend appeared with a gun and said that if she didn't get out he would shoot her. She told him not to be silly and he shot her."

"Any sign of an exit wound?"

She was gently rolled this way and that, with her arm held in position, but no exit wound was to be found. "I'll have to probe the wound under anaesthetic" I said, "could we do her at two o'clock?" "Yes, Doctor." assented Florry.

The operating theatre was a simple room, about 15 feet square with a glass roof, a spotlight on a stand, a table with a rubber mattress that could be pumped up and down, and three or four glass fronted metal cabinets of instruments against the walls. There was a small sterilising room attached with a large oblong chrome boiler for instruments, and a huge brass autoclave for the skin towels and operating gowns. It was a magnificent machine with a massive hinged lid held in place with mighty screw clamps and a steam pressure dial protruding from the top. Underneath was a six burner primus to generate the steam.

At two o'clock I stood beside the table, scrubbed up and in mask, cotton cap, gown and rubber gloves. Butler began to drip ether onto the Schimmelbusch mask over the woman's face and she was soon asleep.

I pulled a bit of blood-stained fabric out of the wound and inserted my finger. The bullet's track passed through the head of her humerus, or where the head of her humerus should have been, and almost came to the surface just below her collar bone. As I couldn't reach any further and I could feel bits of splintered bone, I made an incision there to remove the splinters, but there was no sign of the bullet. The hole it had made disappeared downwards and backwards towards her shoulder blade. "Roll her over again, towards me." I said. Butler clung onto the face mask as the nurses rolled her over. Her back looked perfectly all right, she was not having any trouble breathing so her lungs were intact. Where on earth was this bullet? Following the direction it must surely have taken I felt carefully round her shoulder blade which also seemed perfectly normal, then straightened up to stretch my back, puzzled. I walked a little further towards her spine with my fingertips. "Hello: what's this?"

She seemed to have an extra knob alongside her spine between her shoulder blades; something hard wobbled underneath it. I made a quick incision over the knob and there was the bullet. It must have passed between her shoulder blade and her chest wall and lodged against the spinous processes of her backbone.

When I had managed to work the bullet out of the hole, I had a careful look at it. It was about one and a half inches long, made of a piece of lead sheet rolled together to make a sausage the best part of an inch in diameter, with a bit of bone stuck into one end. I left some rubber drains in the incisions I had made, and in the entry wound, and the nurses dressed them with plenty of cotton wool to soak up the expected juices. The patient was returned to the ward where she was given large doses of penicillin and streptomycin by injection to try and control the infection that would inevitably follow such a wound by a low velocity projectile.

After checking all the other patients I slipped the bullet into my pocket and took it home to show Celia. While we were drinking tea, a Basuto policeman, smart in khaki and with the side of his slouch hat turned up, arrived carrying an ancient gun. "This is what the lady was shot with, *Morena*, we thought you should see it."

It was a short muzzle loading musket, with "Tower 1876" imprinted on the lock. It had a hammer which could be cocked back, and a steel nipple for the percussion cap. There was a ramrod underneath for pushing the slug in on top of the powder.

"Good heavens, this is a Victorian Tower musket. It's nearly a hundred years old. Are these guns still used here?

"Yes *Morena*. They are quite common. Mr Lee says please can he have the bullet?"

"Wait a bit, I must have a photo of this alongside a ruler, no-one

70

would ever believe that people were still firing this sort of thing. It's huge."

Really I should have asked Butler to X-ray the patient's shoulder before operating, but the weather had been appalling and I thought it might be unwise to expose her to the rigours of the cold and snow on the way to the X-ray hut. The next day the weather cleared. The snow had stopped and it was possible to carry her across on a stretcher and take a picture of her shoulder. This was no simple matter, as before Butler could develop the picture, he had to pour the developer into a bucket and heat it up over a primus. The fixer could be used cold. Drying the film took some time, but finally we had a picture.

It showed that the head of her humerus had completely disintegrated. There was no top end to the bone, just fragments. This was lucky for her, as smashing the bone must have taken most of the energy out of the bullet, so that it skidded round her back instead of penetrating her chest. Not so lucky in that her arm would be quite useless. "I'm afraid you will never be able to lift that arm again" I told her before she went home, when all the infection had settled down.

The boyfriend had been found by the police wandering around the hillside in a daze, still clutching the gun. He said that he had been sitting in the hut when a strange smell had wafted in from the fire and he could remember nothing more.

This intrigued me. The story was so odd that it might just be true. Was there any drug or hallucinogen around that perhaps someone had thrown on the fire that might have this effect? What about the thorn-apple, which grew in abundance on the hillside and contained hyoscyamine; that could be hallucinogenic. So I collected some, and brought it home. When I had everything arranged to my satisfaction, I made a small charcoal fire in a metal dish and threw the leaves onto it. I called Celia to sit beside me as I clutched another ancient rifle and inhaled the smoke as it curled off the smouldering leaves.

"Don't worry, the gun isn't loaded," I reassured Celia. "I just wanted to see if inhaling this stuff made me want to shoot you."

"Whatever you say," she replied with a sigh. She had long given up being surprised at some of my antics.

After breathing the noxious fumes for a few minutes I began to develop a frightful headache. Overcome with a fit of coughing, I dropped the gun and staggered out into the open air. I had not had the least desire to shoot my new wife. Just a desperate need to inhale some clean mountain air before I passed out.

When he calmed down, the boyfriend turned out to be a model prisoner. I thought at first that he might be schizophrenic, but the only slightly odd thing he did while in gaol was to collect with great care all his fingernail clippings and hair trimmings. Apparently this was not unusual in Basutoland and merely meant that he did not want to be drawn back to that place by leaving anything of himself behind. In due course he was flown to Maseru for trial.

Several weeks later, when we were seeing patients in the dispensary, a woman walked in. I did not recognise her, but Butler said "This was the woman you took the bullet out of."

"Ask her how her arm is, would you Butler?"

"*Morena!*" she cried, lifting the affected arm high in the air with a bright smile. It was quite extraordinary; she did not appear to have any disability at all.

How on earth could she raise her arm so well when her shoulder joint had been completely shattered? She must have developed a false joint of some kind or she could never have done that.

Butler and I just looked each other and shrugged. Amazing people these Basuto. Still, sometimes it is nice to be proved wrong.

CHAPTER 9
PETER ARRIVES

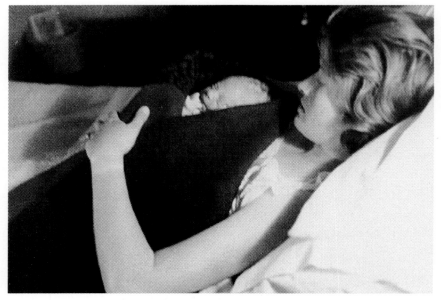

Peter, just born

It was a wonderful summer in the mountains. The Orange River ran low and clear, fed by tinkling streams down the mountain sides, the sky was deepest blue. A colony of storks had settled in the wood at the head of the valley and someone said they had seen a *Lammargier*, the biggest eagle in the world.

The little town was running smoothly. The District Commissioner was in his office catching up with the paper work; Father Michael was to be seen trekking around the District with the bread and the wine in his saddlebags, but always returning to the little church for Communion on Sundays. Brian Lee was in his office, receiving report from his troops of mounted policemen who kept an eye on what was going on in the remote villages. Prisoners from the little gaol were working in the quarry (wherein it was said women of bad repute lurked for the comfort of the convicts) or in peoples' gardens, or driving the twin oxen night soil wagon round to empty the latrines, or on the roads under the watchful eye of the Public Works Officer. The Post Office, Agricultural and Veterinary offices were humming quietly away, people came and went from the gold mines of Johannesburg, the hospital was behaving itself....

And Celia's baby was a fortnight overdue. She was feeling fine in herself, but getting fed up with carrying her great tummy around with no apparent end in sight. I had been trained by Mr Gibberd of Guy's, and had his text book to hand; Mr Gibberd did not believe in intervening for "post maturity" as it often did more harm than good, and in any event nobody could be sure of predicting the date of delivery correctly. The baby would arrive in its own good time and it was simply a matter of waiting. Unless the baby showed some signs of distress there was nothing to be done.

So we waited.

The Sunday morning was glorious, the doves were cooing and the mountains beaming all round. Even the bulk of Mount Sauer across the other side of the valley with his mighty lions paws of foothills seemed slightly ethereal and full of goodwill. Feeling proud and slightly self-conscious, I took Celia by the hand, and together we set off to walk the couple of hundred yards to the little church for Holy Communion.

On the way Celia felt a twinge in her tummy. Nothing severe, so we carried on and took Communion from the hands of Father Michael with most of the other ex-patriates. As we walked home the pains were a little more marked, coming every twenty or thirty minutes.

Celia had had her antenatal care under Jack Smith, down in Matatiele. She found his old fashioned courtesy and punctiliousness quite delightful. He carefully left the room while she was getting herself ready for examination and always wore a spotless white gown and sterile gloves. He had a way of making the whole procedure like initiation into some esoteric cult, and she always felt the better for it. It was certainly in marked contrast to my more direct and rumbustious approach. Jack raised astonished eyebrows when Celia said she wanted her baby to be born in Basutoland, where there were few facilities and no European midwives, but she insisted. She had a romantic notion that she wanted her baby born under the British flag, or at least not in South Africa, a country despised by most of the rest of the world at that time.

As it happens her antenatal progress had been uneventful and Jack was evidently reassured by Celia's wide, child bearing hips.

Sunday passed without change, and though the pains were a little stronger during the night, they were still barely perceptible. Little Florry Kalaka, who was a midwife as well as staff nurse, called round to see Celia, as she and I were to manage the labour, and Florry was to deliver the baby when it came.

"You must excuse me, madam, if I seem a little fearful," said Florry.

"Why, what on earth is there to be fearful about?" Celia asked.

"I have delivered lots of babies, but this is my first white one. This is quite exciting for me, but I am a little fearful that I should do everything right."

"Don't worry, Florry; as far as I know white babies are just the same as black ones", said Celia, reassuringly.

Florry relaxed and bustled around in her crisp white uniform, while I examined Celia internally. I could feel that the cervix was flat and would just admit the tip of my finger. I could just reach the base of the baby's head from above and push it against the finger tips below.

"She's in labour all right, and the head is well down, Florry, but it looks as if it's going to be a long job. How's her blood pressure?"

Florry pumped up the cuff and listened carefully to Celia's arm with the stethoscope. "A hundred and ten over seventy," she said.

"OK, what about her urine?" Florry bustled out to the kitchen where she had set up virtually the only laboratory the hospital possessed, a bottle of Fehling's solution and a spirit lamp. After a while she re-appeared. with the test tubes. "No sugar or protein," she reported, offering them to me for confirmation.

And Monday passed with little change.

On Tuesday the procedure was repeated, and this time Celia's cervix would definitely admit one finger. This was distinctly more open than the previous day, but what an astonishingly slow rate of progress! The trouble was that if Celia walked about the pains came on strongly enough to make her want to lie down, and if she lay down they seemed to stop altogether. Still she was perfectly well and happy, just in no hurry.

"I think we should ring Jack Smith and get his advice," I said. The plan was that Celia should be transferred to the hospital in Matatiele if she got into difficulties.

"But I don't want a Republican baby, I want a Basuto one!"

"All right, don't panic! But I would feel better with a second opinion."

I cranked the handle of the old Swedish phone and was soon put through. After hearing the tale, Jack's advice was that if everything was in order, carry on. He didn't see any reason to bring Celia down, much to her relief.

Despite Celia's leisurely labour, the work of the hospital had to go on, and clinics had to be visited.

There was a young woman in the hospital who had been there ever since I arrived. She had been out walking during one of the spectacular thunderstorms that clatter and burn round the mountains from time to time, and a bolt of lightning had struck so close that it had given her third degree burns down most of her left side. She was lucky she wasn't killed, but when the burns healed there was a cuirass of white scar tissue around the side of her chest and upper thigh, and her left arm was tethered to her side.

I was trying to give her at least some mobility of her arm, by cutting the scar tissue in her armpit, suspending her arm in a sling from a rough gantry above the bed, and covering the exposed flesh with postage stamp split-skin grafts from her thigh. When the grafts were healed the process was repeated. By this time her shoulder was almost up to a right angle and she was beginning to look like a surreal chess board with alternating black and white patches. It was all taking an incredibly long time; she had already been in the hospital for a year and a half. This did not seem to bother her and I marvelled at her unconcern and good humoured patience.

There was a policeman who had smashed the head of his right radius when he fell off his horse. When I was working at Whipp's Cross hospital in Leytonstone I was taught that if the head of the radius was broken into many fragments it should be removed, as the elbow works pretty well without it and if you leave it alone severe osteoarthritis sets in, so I took it out. When I showed it to the policeman the next day, he thought he was being offered a sweet and popped it in his mouth, though he retrieved it for a closer look when he saw my horrified expression.

"Please could you order some more toilet rolls, doctor?" said Florry as I paused on the hospital *stoep* before returning home. "We have only a few left."

Running out of toilet rolls was something that didn't bear thinking about.

"How many, do you think?" I replied.

"Twenty dozen will be enough".

"OK; I'll write to Maseru".

Wednesday dawned without any sign of a baby; I examined Celia to find that her cervix would now admit three fingers. "A finger a day keeps the doctor away" I thought ruefully, but progress was progress.

I had to fly to Mashai for the Wednesday morning clinic. "Don't worry, I'll be fine with Florry and Elsie to look after me," Celia told me as I drove off to the airstrip.

The Dornier was waiting at the strip as I pulled up by the little tin hut that served as an air terminal. Vossie was sitting on one of the wheels, smoking a cigarette.

"Two problems!" he said. "One, we have a following wind off the strip and two, the batteries are low in juice. I'll have to swing her. Do you know how to work the magnetos?"

"No idea at all!"

"OK, then, just climb up beside me. You see these two switches? Well, they operate the magnetos which give the engine the sparks to make it go. You must make sure they are off, like they are now, while I turn her over to suck a bit of petrol in, and when I say CONTACT, you switch them on. It's quite simple, but you mustn't switch them on before I call as the propeller will chop me up. You got it?"

He jumped down and grasped the propeller. "You leave those switches alone till I say!" He pulled the propeller down firmly and stepped back. It plopped across half a turn, wobbled and stopped. He did this again twice. "CONTACT!" he shouted and I pressed the switches down. This time he grasped the propeller firmly with both hands, lifted one foot into the air and threw it down again as he hauled down on the blade, and the engine roared into life.

Vossie clambered up into his seat and shut the door. "We're going to need all the strip we can get," he said, easing open the throttle and trundling the plane to the end. With the rudder hard over he blasted the tail round and thundered down the strip. "Hang onto your hat," Vossie shouted above the row, "The wind's behind us but it's not so strong. We'll probably be all right."

I gritted my teeth as we accelerated down the incline towards the cliff at the end of the airstrip. The little plane shot over the edge, swooped down fifty feet or so, picked up speed and climbed steadily until the peaks were below us. When my pulse settled I relaxed and enjoyed the wonderful panorama of peaks, and in twenty minutes we were bumping along the top of the plateau at Mashai.

The clinic was as straightforward as such clinics ever are, and one patient had to be flown back to Qacha's Nek. The return flight was uneventful and I drove Vossie back to the house for lunch and a gossip; there was always a hunger for news from Maseru.

Celia's condition was apparently unchanged. She still had pains when she stood up which faded when she lay down, and she was still feeling fine.

That evening there was a great thrashing of wings as the stork population rose from the wood *en masse* and flew off down the Orange River valley. We were rather discouraged by this turn of events. Elsie cooked us one of her massive omelettes for supper. The generator which served the hospital and the house was normally switched off at ten o'clock,

Florry Kalaka

but I remembered to ask for it to be left running in case anything happened during the night.

Thursday was day five, and true to form, Celia's cervix admitted five fingers, but her labour pains, though more frequent, were no stronger. Everyone was beginning to get a little fed up, and Florry had the bright idea of asking me to take Celia for a ride in the car along the bumpiest roads I could find.

This was quite effective, and at last Celia's pains began to settle in strongly, one every five minutes. At about ten o'clock that night her waters broke and she began some serious pushing. Florry was there to gentle out the crowning head, but just as the baby was beginning to emerge, all the lights went out. I had remembered to ask for the generator to be left on every night that week except the one when the baby was born.

Fortunately my sailing experience came to our aid and I had made sure the hurricane lamps were filled and trimmed, so we were able to make some light quite quickly, though only just in time for the baby to slither out. Florry's round face was a picture of delight as she tied and cut the cord, wrapped the little bundle into a brand new Basuto blanket with the black alligator pattern. "He's a boy" she said as she handed him to Celia and stood back.

After a few token yells the baby settled in Celia's arms. It had taken a hundred and eleven hours, but all was well, the baby was fine, and Celia's perineum was intact. Florry tidied up, and when she was happy that everything was in order, said goodnight and slipped out into the dark. Peter, as he was to be called, was as good as gold and everyone slept for the rest of the night.

CHAPTER 10
THE CATARACT

Eyelid retractor

"How much longer are we going to have to put up with that awful smell?"

Celia had just emerged from the front door and was blinking in the afternoon sunlight. Baby Peter was nestling in the crook of one elbow. She sat down on the stone wall that surrounded the terrace.

"Don't forget those youngsters are coming round in a while to play some music."

I gave the primus a few more pumps and poked around in the boiling water of the oil drum with a stick

"Not long now," I replied, "the bones are almost clean." I gave the smelly mess an appreciative stir.

The day before two Basuto policemen had arrived with a bundle of bones in a sack. "Mr Lee asked us to bring these bones round to you to see if you can tell us anything about them. They were found washed up on a bank beside the Orange River this morning".

I was intrigued. By then I had done a number of post mortems on smelly corpses, but this was rather different. When I emptied the sack I found it was a complete skeleton wearing a pair of khaki trousers. There was quite a lot of one leg left and shreds of flesh were attached here and there. I handed the trousers back to the policemen.

The skeleton was big enough to be that of an adult. The pelvis was male in form, the skull had all its teeth and there was no sign of any injury to the bones. I couldn't deduce much else from inspecting the remains. However I could possibly get an idea of how old he was if I could see an epiphyseal line between the end and the shaft of a long bone. Hence the boiling to get rid of the rotten flesh, and hence the appalling smell.

"Right; I think they've boiled long enough. When they are a bit cooler I will move them round the back."

* * *

One thing that had been niggling me for some time was that every now and then somebody would attend the dispensary totally blinded with cataracts. The whitened lens was quite obvious and there was nothing I could do about it. Basutoland was a difficult enough country to live in without being blind as well.

I had heard that removing cataracts was quite easy. I had seen a film at medical school of some outfit that was flying round India popping out twenty or thirty cataracts a day in the most primitive places. When I was last in Maseru the Director of Medical Services told me how they used to take out cataracts and not even bother to sew up the wound in the eyeball. "If you leave a strip of conjunctiva at the top of the incision by cutting upwards, you can slip the lens out of the gap and everything falls back into place," he had said.

Some previous doctor had been removing cataracts at Qacha's Nek, because there was a set of Graefe knives and some special eye forceps and other instruments in one of the operating theatre cabinets. Graefe knives are fine narrow bladed scalpels which should be razor sharp, so I sent them to Johannesburg to have them checked and sharpened as they were far too delicate to sharpen on a stone. By doing this I had more or less committed myself to having a try.

After eighteen months on my own I felt in need of a refresher course and had arranged to go to Baragwanath Hospital near Johannesburg . The Basutoland Government had allowed me leave and arranged for a locum, but I had to pay for the course and our train tickets. We could stay with Uncle Bert. My salary was meagre and we had a number of things we wished to buy for the home, which meant that more than one proper medical textbook would make too big a dent in our budget. I had used up most of the book budget on Hamilton Bailey's *Emergency Surgery*, which didn't leave much left for a book on eyes. In my efforts to find something cheap but useful in the medical bookshop I came across *Aids to Ophthalmology* by a Mr P. McG. Moffatt, Consultant eye surgeon at Moorfields eye hospital, one of the best eye hospitals in the world. My pulse began to quicken when I read that it was first written in 1908 but had been updated in 1957. Eyes don't change much, and this little book spanned eye problems from quite primitive times to the era of antibiotics; perhaps this was what was required for somewhere like Basutoland.

When I turned to the section on cataracts I realised that I had struck gold. This little book, one of the Student's Aids Series, contained just the sort of usable information I needed, so I bought it at once.

* * *

The five young men we were expecting duly arrived, and soon had the valley echoing to the sound of a tin whistle and guitar accompanying wonderful rhythmic songs from Soweto. Celia and I were far too inhibited to get up and dance, which was a pity, because the music cried out for it. Nevertheless it was a wonderful impromptu concert and we were amazed at what joy could be teased out of such simple instruments.

When they had gone I took another look at my drum of bones. Using the salad servers I fished out an upper arm bone.

"Here, Celia, look at this!"

"Are those the salad servers? For heaven's sake!" said Celia, taking them from me. Fortunately the bone was cool enough to hold.

"But look at this! You can see the epiphyseal line between the shaft and the head of the humerus!" I pointed to the edge of the thin disc of cartilage which indicated that he had not finished growing. He was still a

Songs from Soweto

boy, though a big one, perhaps about seventeen years old. Greatly excited by this foray into forensic pathology I rang Brian Lee, the Police Officer, and gave him the news. Brian was not as impressed as I had hoped, but thanked me none the less.

When the last patient had left the Dispensary that evening I riffled through the mail. There was a note from the medical stores department attached to my requisition for twenty dozen toilet rolls. It said "Please insert catalogue number." I scribbled: "Can't find catalogue number," underneath, and sent it back.

"Celia, I've admitted a women with a lovely ripe cataract, and you're going to have to help me take it out," I said later the same evening.

"But I don't know anything about taking out cataracts," she replied.

I was fiddling with an ox eye that I had set in a bar of soap and put in a box with a hole cut out. It slithered this way and that as I tried to grasp it with the tiny eye forceps. "Not to worry. What we're going to have to do is work out a programme of precisely what has to be done and in the correct order from this book. Then you can tell me what to do next. You're going to have to hold the torch too, as the theatre light is hopeless for this sort of thing." I carried on working on the ox eye. It was surprisingly tough, and extremely difficult to hold still.

So we drew up a list of twenty four separate steps that would have to be taken in succession to do the operation; and a shorter list of things that had to be checked beforehand. When we were satisfied we went to bed. "Pity we don't have any glasses for them, but if it works she would be able to see pretty well through a pinhole in a piece of card, provided it was light enough," I said sleepily.

* * *

The next morning there was an old man on the doorstep, holding a battered felt hat in both hands. "I'm sorry to trouble you, *Morena*, but please could I have my son back."

I was dumbfounded. What on earth was he talking about?

"Your son?"

"Yes *Morena*. He was found in the Orange River and brought to you."

Then it dawned on me. He was talking about the skeleton I had been boiling. In my enthusiasm to find out how old he was, it hadn't really crossed my mind that this pile of bones was a person. His son! The old man's grief was etched on his face. Life was so hard in Basutoland anyway, and to lose a fine strapping lad as this who could have looked after him in his old age must have been terrible, quite apart from the dreadful loss of a loved one.

"How do you know it is your son?" I faltered.

"They were his trousers," said the old man, simply.

I gathered up the bones as reverently as I could, replaced them in the sack and handed them over. "I'm so sorry......"

"Thank you *Morena*," said the old man as he hoisted the pathetic bundle on his back and trudged off. I remained where I was, staring after him.

* * *

The operating theatre was beginning to feel quite homely. The primuses were roaring, the autoclave hissing, sunlight was pouring through the skylight, Butler Panyane was sitting on his stool at the head of the operating table, though no ether would be required today. Florry was scrubbed up, a ward attendant was fishing instruments out of the steriliser with long tongs and putting them on a sterile towel, and Celia was standing by with a piece of paper and a torch.

I put a pad over the eye that was to be left, cleaned round the other one with Cetavlon, and covered everywhere else with sterile towels. Following Celia's instructions I froze the eye with cocaine drops, and followed these with adrenaline drops to shrink the blood vessels and make bleeding less likely. Then I injected some xylocaine into the facial nerve as it crosses the neck of the mandible, and into the upper and lower eyelids. A stoic like all Basuto, the woman did not move. Finally I injected some more xylocaine behind the eye, and some into the tendon of the muscle on top of the eyeball. Now her eye was blind, paralysed and insensible to pain. I could go ahead.

I passed a stitch through the upper and lower lids and clipped the ends to towels to hold them apart, and another through the muscle on top to hold the eyeball as still as possible.

"Light's wandering!" I said as Celia was reading from the script. It was difficult for her to keep the torch pointing at precisely the right spot and read at the same time.

"*Grasp the medial rectus with forceps and make an incision just outside the cornea at ten o'clock, pass the blade in front of the iris and out at two o'clock and with a gentle to and fro movement of the knife cut up into the upper conjunctiva.*"

Still following the instructions I laid down the knife, caught hold of the iris with forceps and cut a segment out with fine scissors. With the cystitome, a little angulated javelin, razor sharp, I scratched a large triangle on the face of the lens and massaged the lower cornea until the white, useless lens popped out through the hole in the iris.

I carefully tucked the remains of the iris back in place, rinsed out where the lens had been with saline solution and fastened the cornea back in place with tiny stitches. It only remained to remove the various restraining stitches, drop in some atropine and albucid eyedrops, tape the upper eyelid down, cover and pad the eye, and wait.

"So far so good" I smiled to Celia and the staff. "Thank you everyone, now we just have to wait and see if it has worked." After such concentration I wasn't sure whether I was tired or elated.

After a week of careful nursing in the darkest corner of the ward the pad was finally removed. With a big smile the patient said something in Sesuto and pointed at my ginger beard.

"What's she saying?" I asked.

"I can see the doctor, he's all red!" translated Florry.

At least she could see something, which was an improvement on being totally blind. I pierced a postcard with a pin, and she could see quite clearly through the hole. If only we had cataract glasses; but we hadn't.

CHAPTER 11
LETTING OUT AN EVIL SPIRIT

Trephine saw

Qanzi was fond of joala, fermented millet beer, rather like thin, pink, fizzy porridge.

It was wonderful stuff as it tasted good, filled your belly and made you happy at the same time.

There were huge quantities of joala available at the party to lubricate the speeches and songs, but when the moon was beginning to slide down the sky it was time to go home. Qanzi had a new stallion, his pride and joy, but young and scarcely broken. He staggered across to where it was grazing on the sparse grass, and managed to undo the knee-halter, straightened up and tried to lean on the shiny flank but the horse would curvet and sidle around, snorting and showing the white of its eye, which made leaning difficult.

His brother-in-law appeared and held the horse's head while Qanzi tried to calm the agitated beast. After a while he reached up, grasped the pommel, hoisted his left foot into the stirrup, and after hopping about on his other leg for half a minute, managed to swing himself up into the saddle with a bump. By then several other people, awakened by the noise, had gathered round, but the bump was enough to set the nervous animal bolting and Qanzi still hadn't managed to put his right foot in the stirrup. An excellent horseman normally, in his drunken state he could neither control the half-crazed animal, nor maintain his balance. He lurched back and forth, swayed to and fro, and a sudden change of direction threw him off the horse's near side, with his left foot through the stirrup.

The horse bolted on and the foot was still jammed in the stirrup with Qanzi hanging upside down, so that his head was battered against several passing rocks and by the time the other villagers had finally brought the sweating, trembling horse to a halt, Qanzi was deeply unconscious. *They released him, placed his inert form onto a sheet of corrugated iron, picked it up four to a side and set off on the three hour trek to the hospital.*

Eventually the tattered procession arrived with their inert burden; a stretcher was brought and he was carried into the ward and put to bed. I was called to look at him, and meanwhile Florry Kalaka had managed to extract the story from the exhausted men. I looked him over carefully from top to toe; no bones broken or serious injury. I shouted in his ear and pinched his Achilles tendon, but there was no response.

Beyond the fact that he was deeply unconscious, and therefore suspended between life and death, there was little to find except a few bumps and grazes on his head. His pupils were equal and reacted to light, there were no localising neurological signs, his breathing and heart rate were normal, his blood pressure slightly raised, so there seemed to be little to do but set up a slow intravenous dextrose saline drip for some fluid and nourishment since he couldn't be fed by mouth, turn him on his side in case he vomited, keep a regular check on his pulse, temperature and blood pressure, and await events. I was wondering what else might be done, when there was a sudden disturbance.

"*Morena, morena ngaka!* Can you come quickly! There is a man on top of the partition between the lavatories and he won't come down." Florry Khaketla, usually so cool and self assured, was distinctly agitated. The entourage followed her from Qanzi's bedside to the toilet block with as much dignity as it could muster.

There was indeed a man crouched on top of the white painted partition. He was clearly frightened; he appeared tangled in his calico gown with one arm out of the neck hole and he was crouching like a cat, muttering and shouting by turns.

"What on earth is he doing up there?" I cried, realising instantly that it was a stupid thing to say.

"You admitted him last night with gastritis," the nurse replied. " He had settled in well and was feeling a bit better this morning, but just a few minutes ago we noticed his bed was empty, and now he's up there.

"Keep calm everyone" I said, as that is what you say when you are in a crisis and feeling far from calm. "See if you can talk him down. He looks terrified, and if we get excited it will only make him worse. Let's all leave him to it for a bit while we decide what to do. He can't come to much harm up there" I added, hopefully.

"Acute confusional state," said my brain, "What are the causes?" I remembered snippets of my training at Guy's. *Causes for acute confusion could be Psychological, Infective, Surgical, Malignant, Degenerative, or Biochemical.* Was that right? None seemed to apply here anyway. The fellow hadn't been particularly ill, just suffering from a bit of bellyache; he hadn't been operated upon; nothing had happened to upset him, apparently. It was a bit quick for something like a tumour of the brain to come on. What could have happened so suddenly? Was it something we had done?

"Lets have a look at his charts." Florry unhooked the charts from the end of his bed and passed them to me. His temperature was normal, his pulse rate had risen a bit for some reason, there was no other comment.

"Medication? What's he on?"

"Magnesium trisilicate mixture half an ounce three times a day, and tincture of belladonna.".

"How much belladonna?" I enquired.

"Half an ounce three times a day as well." she replied.

"HALF AN OUNCE?" I exclaimed. " The dose is ten minims, that's ten drops, three times a day! No wonder he's gone crackers; the poor chap's hallucinating!"

"But what do we do?" said nurse.

"How many doses has he had?

"Only one, at eight o'clock. The dispensary didn't open until this morning."

"Well, it's getting on for noon, so with a bit of luck it will be wearing off by now. Set one of the ward attendants to keep an eye on him, to see he doesn't hurt himself. I'll come and see what's going on after lunch."

When I returned after lunch, the man had come down from the partition and he was feeling much better. Qanzi's condition was unchanged and everyone else in the hospital seemed happy enough. I had decided it was time we had an afternoon off and Michael Hardy had offered the loan of the mission horses for a diamond sieving expedition. Peter was tucked happily on Elsie's back, swathed in her Basuto blanket, so we felt it would be all right to set off. Our little expedition trotted out of town, the half hour or so's ride down a steep incline, past the cliff down which some ingenious thieves had thrown the District Commissioners safe, causing it to burst open, and we dismounted beside one of the many streams that fed the Orange river.

Keith Whitelock and his gang of diamond diggers had sieved practically every stream in the country looking for the tell-tale chips of ilmenite (black) garnet (red) and olivine (green) that indicated diamond-bearing kimberlite somewhere upstream. Watching the sieve for the coloured gleams of these semi-precious stones while swirling it in the stream was both exciting and absorbing. In theory, one might find a diamond too, but we didn't, though we did find a few garnets.

Happy and tired, we ambled home to supper and a quiet evening. Baby Peter had been as good as gold on Eslie's back, and went to sleep

Basuto horsemen

after his evening feed. It had been a good day.

Thanks to careful nursing, Qanzi gradually came round over the next few days, but his left leg remained stiff and paralysed, suggesting the probability that damage to his brain was paralysing his leg. This was the sort of situation that the blessed saint Hamilton Bailey might cover, so I fetched down his wonderful *Emergency Surgery* to see what he had to say on the matter. As I leafed through his pages I wondered why the government didn't supply a decent range of text books; they could be a great comfort, as well as increasing our meagre skills enormously.

Hamilton Bailey's marvellous book did not quite cover Qanzi's situation, but it did say that if the diagnosis was not clear: *It is this uncertainty that heartens one in advising a comparatively atraumatic operative procedure, which will clarify the diagnosis, may prove life saving and can do no harm.* I read it again. Surely he was talking about making a hole in someone's head. *An atraumatic procedure?* How extraordinary. One would have thought that making holes in someone's head was rather dangerous and might do quite a lot of harm. But if Hamilton Bailey says it's all right and there is some chance of relieving Qanzi's paralysis, I supposed I should give it a try.

Over the years all sorts of instruments had gathered in the operating theatre cupboards, including a trephine set, with a "T" shaped handle that engaged with a number of circular cutters, like upside-down crowns, of different sizes. The one about an inch in diameter looked about right, and I asked for the whole kit to be boiled up.

Exploratory burr holes are made under local analgesia. Really? without even putting the patient to sleep? *Upwards of four of these explorations may be necessary to exclude a surgically remediable lesion.* Four seemed rather a lot. My courage might just run to two, one on each side of his head in the region of the motor cortex, well above the dreaded arteries of the temporal region.

So it was that a couple of hours later, with Qanzi's head cradled in my arm, I was grinding a hole in his skull, tilting the handle of the trephine from time to time to see if the disc of bone was coming loose. After all, it required quite a lot of pressure to keep the saw biting and one wouldn't want to push the whole thing into his head.

Qanzi was as good as gold. He had not raised the slightest objection to an injection of local anaesthetic into his scalp and a deep incision. I tied off a few bleeding points with catgut and cranked the incision open with special locking forceps, exposing the white bone of the skull. Qanzi was chattering away as the spirit moved him when eventually the disc of bone came loose, exposing the dura, the tough membrane that covers the brain. Following Hamilton Bailey's instructions, I carefully cut a cross in the tight membrane, revealing a perfectly normal looking brain, with no sign of raised pressure or blood. I probed carefully around between his skull and the surface of his brain in case there was a clot nearby, but there was nothing. Rather disappointed, I replaced the disc of bone, stitched up the scalp with a short rubber drain protruding from the wound to let out any fluids that might build up, and taped a dressing over the top.

I repeated the procedure on the other side, and this time the dura was dark, and incision produced a few drops of red blood, but again there was no evidence of a clot, so I replaced the disc and sewed up the scalp.

That night Qanzi went slightly crazy, removed his dressings and pulled out his drains, but the nurses calmed him down and bandaged him up again.

His recovery from the trephining was otherwise perfectly straightforward; it was almost as if nothing had happened to him. Furthermore over the next few days his leg woke up, and in a couple of weeks he walked out of the hospital unaided.

Maybe it was a coincidence; there was no way of knowing for sure, but it made me think about those pictures of prehistoric skulls which show evidence of having been trephined in life. Perhaps thousands of years before a shaman had had a similar patient, made a hole in his head to let out the evil spirit and the patient had recovered?

90

CHAPTER 12
THE HAND

Vossie's Dornier

The sound of the wind roaring through the pinions of several mountain vultures as they wheeled and dived at us was disturbing, if not actually terrifying. I was climbing a moderately difficult rock face with Keith and Irene Whitelock high up on the lip of the escarpment, a few miles from Qacha's Nek along the dirt road to Sekake's.

Keith was a first class climber and explorer, and we had been on several outings together on rock faces in the neighbourhood. There was one pillar of sandstone a mile or so outside the camp which I had climbed on my own. As the top of the rock sloped away I had had to rely on a single friction hold with one foot, and I was not roped. I told Keith about it expecting to be praised for this remarkable ascent.

"A totally unjustified move," was his response, "and a stupid one."

I was glad to be invited to climb with them again this time. It was a beautiful day, and when we reached the top I felt so triumphant that I roared out some German ballads I had learned for the house singing competition at school; "*Ich grolle nicht, und wenn das Herz auch bricht........*" I shouted to the sky and the hills and valleys. When I had quite finished Keith gave me a quizzical look: "Aren't you just glad to be here?" he said. Crestfallen, I sat down and shut up. I think he found my attitude rather trying.

The escarpment which formed the eastern border of Basutoland was

91

a feature to be reckoned with. Seen from the air while flying back from Durban, it stretched like a row of blue and jagged teeth from horizon to horizon rising several thousand feet out of the plain. In clear sunlight the peaks were smiling and wonderful, but when the wet wind blew up them from the lower ground of the Republic, they could suddenly disappear into cloud, rain and snow.

In certain conditions the cloud layer would remain stationary while the wind streamed up through it, and it seems that that was what had disorientated a light aeroplane flying home into Basutoland in bad weather a few weeks before. Suddenly losing visibility, the pilot had tried to turn back, but in the course of the turn had flown smack into a vertical rock face, killing himself and his fiancée instantly.

I had been called to the scene, but clambering up the track had met the mounted police detachment riding down with the remains of the couple in saddlebags. I was required to do a post mortem, but there was only a female pelvis and the diagonal half of the man left, so my report was rather short. This pilot had already had 10,000 hours experience flying in the Republic, but the Republic was mostly flat and mountains have a completely different set of rules and challenges.

Generally flying among the mountains was wonderful; often thrilling and at times terrifying. The skill of the Basutair pilots was quite extraordinary. I was lucky enough to have to fly somewhere practically every week in one or other of their little four-seaters. They had a couple of Cessnas, graceful and powerful; three Piper Tri-pacers squat and homely on their sit-up-and-beg tricycle undercarriage, a couple of business-like Dorniers with blue and white livery and fat wings, and a buff-coloured Lockheed Lhasa, a kind of flying biscuit tin with plenty of power and lots of space inside, but absolutely no grace at all.

The airstrips were scattered all around the little country, some more or less flat, though maybe on top of a plateau, like the one at Mashai, or a sodden elevated valley like the one at Simonkong. Some, on the other hand, sloped uphill and even tilted sideways as well, so that the little planes stopped after a few yards, but then had to roar frantically up the strip before they could take off for the return flight. Often they had to land in a cross wind, coming in like a crab and straightening out at the last minute. Vossie had even invented his own way of landing in a cross wind if there was room; he would land in an arc so that the tendency of the wind to flip the windward wing upwards was counteracted by the tendency of the plane to roll the other way. Some of the strips were flat all right, but they had a hill at one or both ends, so the pilots had to sideslip down to lose altitude when they were landing. When they took off again they would climb steeply out at a speed that would have led to a fatal stall, if they hadn't been able to creep over the ridge and thunder down the valley at the other side.

Still tingling from a particularly memorable flight from the little clinic in a rondavel on the plateau at Mashai, I was having tea with Celia on the *stoep* when the phone rang. It was Florry. "Doctor, there is a lady with a prolapsed arm and I can't deliver her, can you come, please?"

The baby had been dead for a long time. Its poor little blue arm was protruding from its exhausted mother's vagina. I had a terrible premonition that this was going to be too much for me, but I had to try and sort the situation out. I was briefly struck by the thought of this little baby groping for the light it would never see, but there was no time for such speculation. The baby was dead and its mother not far behind.

"Let's put up a dextrose saline drip; she's dehydrated and ketotic from lack of nourishment," I said. "Have a bottle of Dextran ready to follow."

"May I start, please Mr Mohapeloa?" I asked when all was ready and the patient asleep after only a few breaths of ether. Mr Mohapeloa was standing in for Butler Panyane.

Her womb wasn't far below the surface of her distended abdomen, and the flesh parted like butter at the stroke of my scalpel. Another gentle scalpel stroke into the womb itself and the baby was revealed. "Ergometrine injection now, please nurse" I said.

I grasped a leg, and apart from a slight resistance as the head disengaged the limp little body was easily delivered, with his arm trailing behind. There was a certain amount of blood around, but nothing seriously worrying, so I delivered the placenta and sewed up the now contracted womb. For the first time I was beginning to hope; it had been so much easier than I had expected that I was even humming to myself.

But my relief was short lived. "Her pulse is weakening; she's bleeding *per vaginam*" said dispenser and nurse almost simultaneously.

So she was. Blood was pouring from her. Hastily putting in the last abdominal stitches, I thrust my right fist into her vagina and pressed down on the womb with my left hand. The bleeding stopped, but not before she had lost a good three pints of blood. There was blood everywhere.

Withdrawing my hand, I straightened my aching back and tried to think coherently. This woman was going to die unless I did something. The bleeding had stopped and she was having copious intravenous fluids to try and make up for her lost blood, but she was still unconscious despite the fact that Mr Mohapeloa had stopped administering ether some time before. Her pulse was rapid and barely palpable. Nurses, dispenser were all looking at me.

"Blood!" I said. "She needs blood; that's the only thing that can

93

possibly save her! they usually have a bottle of O negative blood in Matatiele, I'll try and beg it from them. There's nothing else I can do here. Phone them that I'm on my way. I'll be back as soon as I can."

It was a forlorn hope, but it was with a terrific feeling of relief that I ran to the Land Rover and roared off into the gathering dark up to the border gate. They might not have any blood at the little hospital in Matatiele, and might not give it to me if they had, but anything was better than simply standing by and watching her die.

I slithered to a halt at the border gate and hooted, but no policeman appeared to unlock it, so I dashed into the police hut, to find the policeman on duty unrousable and apparently drunk. There was no sign of a key. I grabbed the telephone handset on the wall and churned the handle. After a maddening pause a sleepy voice answered.

"This is the border gate and I can't rouse the man on duty to get out, I have to get to Matatiele as soon as possible to fetch some blood!" I said, a mixture of panic and fury rising in my breast.

The border gate

"You must go to the border gate." was the reply.

"No, I am at the border gate and I can't open it!" I said desperately.

"You have to go to the border gate and the policeman will open it for you."

94

I hung up and ran back to the rumbling Land Rover. Engaging the low ratio gear and with engine screaming I charged at the barbed wire border fence to the side of the gate and plunged through.

Bucketing and bouncing down the road, trailing several yards of barbed wire and a few iron stakes behind me, swerving this way and that to avoid rocks and corners as they suddenly appeared in the headlights, required all my concentration and blew away my panic, even filling me with a kind of exhilaration.

In an hour I drew up outside the little hospital where night sister was waiting for me.

"You've got a bit of a cheek, young man expecting us to give you one of our precious bottles of O negative just like that!" she said, in mock severity as she handed the bottle over. "Sure you can't stay for a cup of something?" Her soft South African accent was gentle and reassuring.

"'Fraid not, Sister. Sorry, must get back. You're an angel! I'll bring it back tomorrow if we don't use it". I took the bottle and ran back to the Land Rover.

The drive back was as hazardous as the drive down, but as I drew up outside the hospital, before I went in, I knew what I would find. All the lights were on and there was no sound except the thumping of the generator. Clutching the precious bottle of blood I walked reluctantly up the steps and through the door.

The operating theatre had been scrubbed clean, but the young woman still lay on the table, covered with a white sheet. Mr Mohapeloa rose from his stool at the head of the table. "I'm afraid she died soon after you left" he said.

I suddenly felt completely exhausted. "I can't imagine we'll be needing the theatre again tonight. Could you see that someone takes her to the mortuary first thing tomorrow?"

In a dream I walked home. What on earth was I doing in this place? Were these things really happening? The last few hours had been impossibly unreal. The moon had risen and the mountain peaks looked like cardboard cut-outs. I pulled open the fly screen, opened the door and went to the kitchen. I put the blood in the paraffin fridge, tip-toed to the bedroom, threw off my clothes, hauled on my pyjamas, crawled under the blankets and snuggled up against Celia's back.

"How did you get on?" she asked sleepily.

"Tell you in the morning."

I slept.

CHAPTER 13
HORSES

Off on trek

When I was a boy, living in my parents' preparatory school near Haslemere in Surrey, other people always seemed to have horses, and we had plenty of opportunities to borrow or hire one to go hacking over the moors. My father loved to have a go at things, so he decided to have a go at horses. He reckoned that feeding them would be no problem, as there was plenty of grass on the playing field and surplus bread and puddings from the school with which to top them up. It might even save on the mowing.

He bought a retired polo pony called Rufus, which he kept falling off, as Rufus had only two speeds, flat out and stop. When Rufus stopped, he stopped dead, suddenly, and whoever was on board generally flew off. My elder brother David had a tired old nag, a strawberry roan called

Dart. They did not like each other very much, and soon Dart died of some sort of enteritis and David decided his riding days were over.

I had Nanette.

Now, Nanette was a fierce, black Exmoor pony. She was extremely strong-minded and took a fiendish delight in being uncatchable when she saw a bridle, unless you had a pocket full of bread. She would rear up and wave her hoofs around if frustrated or angry, so I always felt much safer when in the saddle. She had another bad habit, that of suddenly lying down and rolling when you least expected it.

She loved to escape from the field by wriggling through a gap in the hedge, and then there was nothing for it but to wait for news. Once the Mother Superior of the Holy Cross sanatorium, which was just beyond the school playing field, rang to ask us if we would kindly remove our horse as she was walking up and down the open ward and the patients were feeding her grapes. Another time someone from Shottermill rang to say that Nanette was sitting by their kitchen fire and would we please come and fetch her.

She liked to bolt from time to time, especially at gymkhanas, and the only way to stop her was to steer her at a house or a haystack or some other impossible barrier

Despite all this, once she was settled down, she was wonderful to ride over the moors between Haslemere and Hindhead, which were almost treeless and covered with short, crisp heather as they had been used for tank practice in the war, which had reduced the soil to little more than acidic sand. There was nobody about and you could see for miles. I was about twelve years old at that time and a great admirer of Roy Rogers, the singing Hollywood cowboy, who had high eyebrows, so I used to hold my eyebrows high until they ached so much that I had to let them drop. I once saw him perform in the flesh at Earls' Court, with his beautiful white horse Trigger; rather a good act, which ended with them both climbing into a large bed together. When they had been lying still for a while, Trigger would lean over and grab the counterpane with his teeth and haul it on top of himself, leaving the cowboy uncovered, so that he had to get up and try to tug some of it back again.

Living in a school meant that all my friends disappeared at the end of term and I was on my own a great deal, so I rode Nanette for hours over the moors, alone with my thoughts. In the absence of human company she made a pretty good companion.

In due course I went on to public school and Nanette had to be sold. This was sad but inevitable, and I was delighted when she was returned after the first attempt to sell her, as the girl to whom she had been sold couldn't control her.

I vowed that one day I would have another pony like her.

The Basuto appeared to spend much of their lives in the saddle and though the breed had sadly deteriorated due to the massive requirements for remounts in the Boer and the fourteen-eighteen wars, there was a specific Basuto pony. They were small, tough and sure footed and could scramble through the rocky dried out watercourses, or *dongas*, and up the almost vertical sides without shedding their rider. These ponies also had a special gait, called tripling, in which they could run along at about fourteen miles an hour. They were taught this by having their heads held high while they were whacked across the rump with a *sjambok*, a painful but effective method of training. It was far more comfortable for the rider than trotting and the little ponies could keep it up for hours.

The Basuto Mounted Police, on the other hand, had beautiful thoroughbreds, and very fine they looked, too.

"I hear you have been after a pony for some time, Colin," said Johnny Toolan one day when the diamond diggers were in town, "I'm moving on and I can't take mine with me. I'll bring him round so you can take a look at him."

I fell for him at once. He was fourteen hands and as tough as old boots. We called him *Naledi*, because of the white star on his forehead. I fed him on crushed mealies, and kept him in the stable near the house, a relic of former times. He had to be gelded as stallions were not allowed in

Police guard of honour

camp, and he took extreme exception to the procedure. I heard later that he had jumped right over the veterinary officer before they could restrain him.

He was a worthy successor to Nanette, complete with most of her bad habits, including bolting. I was riding along the lip of the cliff that overhung our house, shouting for Celia to come out and look at how dramatic I must appear silhouetted against the sky one evening, when the pony suddenly took off at breakneck speed, slithering about on loose shale near the cliff edge. Fearing disaster I steered him away from the edge towards a tight thicket of small conifers, thinking this would bring him to a halt. Nanette would have stopped, but not Naledi, who crashed straight into it and thrashed on until we were finally brought to a standstill by interlocking branches.

We explored the surrounding hills together, though he did have that irritating habit common to many horses, of pretending to get tireder and feebler until I turned towards home, when he would suddenly perk up, all exhaustion cured. So then I would turn him round again until he would grind almost to a standstill and have to be kicked soundly to keep him going. In the end I bought a *sjambok*, a stiff, rawhide whip, one sight of which out of the corner of his eye, would keep him going.

He was certainly sure-footed, and once when we were descending a steep slope, sat down and glissaded for about forty yards in the scree on his rump. I was astonished, but hung on. He was quite unconcerned, considering this to be a perfectly rational way to proceed, and made no attempt to throw me off.

* * *

"Colin?" said Brian Lee, the Police superintendent one day. "I believe you will be flying up to the clinic at Mashai this morning?"

"That's right."

"While you're there, could you take a look at one of my horses? I've had a radio report that one of them has been found dead in its stable."

"Of course, though I'm not much of a vet."

It was a beautiful flight up, with the shadow of the Cessna on the filmy cloud below us, entirely surrounded by a brilliant rainbow ring.

"Look, there's Vossie in the Dornier" said Tony Clegg, my pilot for the day. "I think he wants a dog-fight."

So we spent the next ten minutes zooming round the sky, but Vossie cunningly positioned himself under our tail. Though the Dornier was slower, however hard Tony twisted and turned we still couldn't see Vossie, while all the time he was watching us through his perspex roof.

"Better get on," said Tony banking, the Cessna away, "we'll be in trouble if anyone sees us behaving like this."

Mashai was in turmoil when we arrived.

The horse was indeed dead. He had sheared off the outer part of his hoof trying to pull it out of the gap between the stable floor and the corrugated iron wall of the stable, and bled to death. Lying alongside the horse was a man, also dead, his head beaten flat.

"What's this? no-one told me a man had been killed?" I enquired.

"He was a bad man, a *tsotsi* from Johannesburg, *Morena*," said the policeman. "Look at his guns."

Two large pistols

He pointed to two huge automatic pistols lying on a nearby shelf. "He came back to his village to show off what a big shot he had become and started waving his guns about at a party. The villagers tried to disarm him so he shot a couple of them before they managed to kill him." Moral: never threaten a Mosuto.

"Shot them dead?"

"No, *Morena*. There is one waiting for you in the clinic and another on the way."

Passing through the usual crowd of blanketed patients sitting patiently on the ground, I opened the door of the little *rondavel* which served as a clinic. Sitting on a chair by the desk was a man with a groove along the top of his head. It wasn't bleeding and he seemed quite unconcerned, so I asked the aide to clean the wound and apply a dressing.

I settled down and managed to see the rest of the patients before there was a commotion outside.

Blinking in the bright sunlight, I saw a man lying on a sheet of corrugated iron with four strong but exhausted men sitting around him. A small crowd gathered. The man looked extremely ill.

"Look, *Morena*," said the policeman, lifting his blanket. There was a small hole in his abdomen through which greenish sludge was oozing.

"Perforated gut," I said. We must get him back to Maseru immediately for operation if he is to have a chance of surviving. I will have to commandeer the aeroplane and answer for it afterwards. Could someone bring him across? And could you radio Maseru to have an ambulance at the airport?"

Tony was quite happy to be diverted, and as we flew back over the mountains, I suddenly realised that Celia would be expecting me home for tea. The Cessna had no radio, we couldn't let her know. Oh well.

The Land Rover ambulance was waiting when we landed, and our patient extracted from the plane, put on a stretcher and slid into the back with an aide to keep an eye on him. He was still breathing, but unconscious.

* * *

Within the hour he was on the operating table at Queen Elizabeth II hospital, with a drip running and his abdomen open. There were multiple perforations in his smaller intestine and I assisted and mopped while Dr Jacques meticulously oversewed each hole.

When everything was tidy he closed the abdomen in layers and we retired to the changing room to rid ourselves of our gowns and rubber boots, and have a cup of coffee and a rest for a while.

Suddenly I remembered Celia again, leapt up and hurried to the Police station to ask them to send a radio message to Qacha's Nek explaining that I would be flying back the next day.

"Where on earth have you been?" she greeted me on my return. She was quite angry. I had never seen her like this before.

"I'm sorry, but what with one thing and another......"

"I was worried sick because off you went to Mashai, and I heard on the South African radio that there were riots in Maseru which had spread to Mashai, and that someone had been shot dead!".

It briefly crossed my mind to wonder how a riot could spread over eighty miles of impassable mountains.

Just as I was about to launch into the details of the improbable happenings of the last twenty four hours, a Basuto policeman arrived with a piece of paper.

"It's for you, madam," he said, with a salute, and strode off.

Celia pored over it for a while.

"What's this all about?" she said, handing it to me.

It read:

"*PXXLD OFORGU JUNGT NGHII BFROVN UFFIGHE CLOGUNX*

TUESDAY STOP COLIN"

"Today's Wednesday," she continued relentlessly, "and Peter hasn't been at all well. I think he's got a fever. Anything might have happened to you."

I took another look at the message. It was completely incomprehensible, and apart from my name the only legible word was wrong. I wondered if police messages were usually like that.

"Anyway, you're back and in one piece, so that's the main thing. But I was really worried."

"Really worried", I thought. "That's a backhanded compliment of a sort..." I had been trying to make her worry about me on and off since she had arrived eighteen months before, but apparently failed. On one occasion I had found a large flat rock teetering on the edge of a cliff when we were out exploring. If I walked out on it it began to tilt with a groan, but if I jumped back it settled back again. I did this a few times, but found Celia was not even paying attention, let alone worrying about me. "Come back and stop being silly," she had said after a while. Sheepishly, I did so.

She calmed down and became attentive as I unfolded the story of the last twenty four hours.

"Well, I have heard some weird excuses in my time, but that's one of the best. You'll be glad to hear that nothing disastrous has happened in the hospital while you have been away; they mostly seem to happen when you are here. Perhaps you should go away more often."

It sounded as if I was forgiven. I felt quite light hearted as I cranked the telephone in the hope of getting through to the hospital in Maseru to find out how our patient was doing. When the exchanges at Matatiele, Bethlehem, Ficksburg and Maseru had finally connected I had a short talk with the Sister on duty and hung up, giving the handle a final twirl.

"That man we flew in from Mashai........." I paused.

"Yes. How is he?" said Celia.

"Dead. He died soon after the operation."

Oh God, not another death.

We'd failed again.

CHAPTER 14
PELLETS AND LEG BONES

Tibia and fibula

A boy of about twelve had been admitted earlier one afternoon, with a small puncture in his left upper eyelid. His mother and father were sitting on the floor by his bed.

"Ask them what happened, would you, Florry?"

There was a brief exchange in Sesuto. "His friend shot him with an air rifle and the pellet hit him in the eye," she replied.

"Have they got the pellet?"

"They say it must be still in his eye, because it never came out again.."

I examined his eye carefully and checked his eyesight; everything seemed to be fine, and the boy was quite well in himself.

"I think we had better X-ray his head and see where it is. Being lead it should show up well. Could you ask Butler to take his picture, laying the left side of his face on the plate and concentrating on the front part of his skull? That should show up his orbit nicely."

* * *

The phone rang when we were having afternoon tea.

I picked it up and listened, amazed. "Why don't you take him to the vet?" I replied when I had heard the story. "Oh all right, I'll take a look at him. I'll be over in half an hour."

"What was that about?" said Celia.

"The Petersen's dog has been bitten by a baboon and they want me to see it. I'm not sure whether I ought to be flattered or furious. The Veterinary Officer says that pets are nothing to do with him, and the dog

103

would have to be seen to in Matatiele. They doubt if he would make it," I replied.

The little terrier was in a bad way. The baboon had picked him up and bitten the back of his neck through to the bone. He was lying on his side with his eyes half open, so I propped a Schimmelbusch mask on his nose and after two or three drops of ether he was completely unconscious.

I poured some sulphonamide powder into the wound and stitched him up with five deep stitches, leaving plenty of gaps so that any fluid could drain out.

"I don't give much for his chances," I warned them, "he is half dead already, and the other half may not be far behind. He isn't even bleeding."

My forays into veterinary medicine in the past had been dogged by failure. Somehow the Brackenburys of The Ring of Bells, a public house in North Bovey on Dartmoor had persuaded me to try and cure a bloated Shetland pony when we were staying there. It died soon after I had given it a soap and water enema. Similarly a crop-bound chicken had succumbed after I had tried to massage the blockage clear. My only success was buying some warts off one of their retired steeplechasers.

My pessimism was justified and the dog died soon afterwards.

* * *

The next day Butler Panyane produced the X-ray of the boy's head. I peered at the outline of his orbit. I could see it quite clearly but there was no pellet there. Could I just make out some tiny flecks of lead behind his eye?

"What about that, doctor?" said Butler pointing right in the middle of the picture. There it was as large as life, the perfect shadow of a waisted .177 lead pellet right in the middle of his head. I had been inspecting his orbit so intently that I had failed to notice it.

"My God, Butler, it has lodged deep in his brain, and it is bound to be infected. We must get him to a neurosurgeon as soon as possible. I will have to requisition a plane and I will go along too to keep an eye on him. We had better give him a cocktail of all the antibiotics we can lay our hands on before he gets meningitis."

The day after was a Saturday. A Tri-pacer duly arrived with Vossie at the controls and we sat the boy in one of the back seats. Fortunately he still seemed to be perfectly well.

The flight to Durban was quite simple, because you could see the dark inverted cone of smog from miles away. The boy seemed to enjoy the flight, and was quite unperturbed when an ambulance came and took him away from the airport to the hospital.

Vossie immediately turned the plane around and we set off for home.

"Why are you hitting the compass?" I asked when we were half way back. "Because it's no bloody good, that's why," he replied, giving it another wallop. Every time he hit it, it said something else, and would budge no further until he hit it again.

My heart sank. I have a recurrent waking dream about being in an aeroplane and there's nowhere to land. The view was far from reassuring. The saw toothed Drakensberg escarpment was stretched out on our right as far as the eye could see; we had flown out between two of those teeth, but which two?

I needn't have worried. "All we have to do is find the railway line and follow it to Matatiele," said Vossie, "then its easy to follow the road up to the pass. That looks like a station over there." He banked and dived down to get a closer look. It was indeed a station and we could see its name on a board as we zoomed past. So we had a perfect navigational fix, and all we had to do was follow the line as it snaked over the arid, brown countryside. The border gate flashed by close under our wheels and we floated down onto the airstrip.

He was off again as soon as I had climbed out of the plane.

It was Saturday night, when some of us used to foregather in the bar of the Maluti Inn to yarn and laugh and swig Castle Lager or Lion Ale until we were quite squiffy. Brian Lee had some hilarious stories of his training with the South African mounted police in Pretoria and we were all eager to hear the latest jokes brought by commercial travellers. A lot of the jokes revolved around a particularly dim Afrikaner called Koos van der Merwe. When Peter was small and wrapped tightly in his little Basuto blanket, we used to take him along and prop him up on one end of the bar, but he was getting a bit too big for that, so Celia tended to stay at home with him and let the boys get on with it.

That evening I came rollicking back with a case of Lager under my arm, lost my way in the dark, stepped off one of the terrace walls in the garden and floated gently to the ground, astonished rather than hurt. I got up and stumbled around to the back of the house, scrambled for a while in the undergrowth, and found myself at the bottom of the sandstone cliff that loomed over it. The moon came out from behind a cloud and I looked at the scene in a kind of ecstasy. I was overwhelmed by the beauty of it all, and the cliff seemed to be bulging and about to burst open like an over-ripe fig. It was some time before I could tear myself away.

"What on earth have you been up to? Look at the state you're in," said Celia severely as I staggered in. "And your supper is cold."

I opened my mouth to try and explain my recent epiphany, but nothing coherent emerged so I closed it again. I knew I was in disgrace and would feel terrible the next morning in church. As it turned out, my prognosis was correct, and it served me right.

* * *

In theatre on Monday morning I was faced with a teenage girl with a bit of loose, dead bone sticking out of an ulcer just above the inside of her left ankle. She had turned up at the dispensary a few days before, smart as paint in a new gym slip. Clearly the piece of bone would have to be removed or the ulcer would never heal. She could walk all right but when we saw her X-ray we were flummoxed. The picture was quite extraordinary; her tibia was over twice the proper width and quite irregular in outline.

Butler soon had her asleep, and Florry and I cleaned up her leg and laid it on sterile towels. I gave the bit of bone a tentative twitch; it slid up and down quite easily, but only for about half an inch, so I decided to follow it up her leg until I could remove it altogether. I nibbled and dug my way up her shin, leaving a longer and longer trough in her leg, but what had seemed like something quite small was extending and getting wider the higher I went. I wasn't able to remove the dead bone completely until I was a few inches below her knee, at which point it had grown from a narrow stick to a complete ring of bone. By the time I had finished, I had removed almost her entire original tibia. She had grown a complete new one round the old one; it was fat and irregular, but it worked perfectly well.

I left the wound open, and with careful nursing and dressing it eventually healed up from the bottom, and off she went on her home-made leg.

* * *

As a government Medical Officer I was in charge of everything medical from drains to forensic pathology, and one of my jobs was inspecting the gaol. This was like a small stone castle and though it had leg irons and handcuffs hanging in the gatehouse, I never saw them used. Mr. Christmas, the Prison Officer was a big, cheerful Mosuto who delighted in demonstrating and squashing the bed bugs which were to be found sheltering in crevices in the whitewashed walls. Unsure of my role, I made complimentary noises, and apart from the bugs the place was always clean and tidy, and the prisoners seemed to be well fed and perfectly happy.

In Qacha's Nek you were either sane or a lunatic, so that if you were ill enough physically you went to hospital, but if you were a lunatic you went to gaol. One weekend when I had been away, Tom Lawrence had admitted a lunatic and called in a witch doctor to deal with him. The witch doctor, who was skilled in herbal medicine, prescribed a powerful purge, which gave him such frightful diarrhoea that his mania completely disappeared. He was a very subdued lunatic when I returned, so we could send him back to his village. It occurred to me that this could be useful therapy when we were back in England.

That week I had to a witness a boy being given four strokes with a light cane, which had been ordered by Tom in his role as magistrate, as punishment for some misdemeanour. The prison officer carefully swathed the boy's trunk and upper thighs in folded grey blankets, just leaving his buttocks exposed as he lay face down on the table. Each stroke was delivered with precision with the long cane, leaving a white line on his brown bottom where it had struck. The boy never moved or uttered a cry.

Little harm was done, but this still made me uneasy. The punishment was administered fairly and after proper legal proceedings, but I could not help feeling that, even though I was there to see that the punishment was not overdone, I was still colluding with the powerful against the powerless. What about the doctors in some parts of the world who are asked to witness torture, in theory to make sure it does not go too far, but whose presence could be said to legitimise it? Whose side were they on? When does one protest?

On another occasion a prisoner was brought to the dispensary with both lower arms paralysed, because his upper arms had been tied too tightly behind his back, apparently crushing the circumflex humeral nerves, whilst in Police custody. I noted the case, wrote a short report for Brian Lee, and said I thought he would probably recover in due course. In retrospect maybe I should have made a fuss and reported the matter to somebody outside the district, but I was quite unprepared for such situations, and had no idea where my duty lay.

* * *

The boy with the pellet in his brain was returned to us after a couple of weeks on antibiotics, and promptly developed meningitis and had to be flown back to Durban.

The neurosurgeons there had hoped that the boy would get better without intervention, which was clearly not the case. So this time they patched the hole in his orbit somehow with a bit of his temporal muscle. After more antibiotics, the meningitis settled down, he was flown back again, and we were able to send him home fully recovered. We were very fortunate to be able to call upon such expertise from time to time, though we could only send those few patients who were not urgent and were fit enough to travel.

* * *

A letter was waiting for me when I sat down to see the patients in dispensary one evening. I opened it.

"What do you think of this Butler. You remember the toilet rolls we sent for?"

"Yes doctor, we couldn't find the catalogue number."

"They have returned our requisition with a note attached, saying 'Catalogue number is 5053, please insert', so I suppose we had better do that and send the wretched thing back again." So I did.

To my surprise the first patient was our Elsie.

"*Morena*, sometimes I am very tired and find it difficult to breathe," she said.

She never complained at home, but when I listened to her heart I heard the unmistakable to-and-flow roar of aortic stenosis. She must have had rheumatic fever at some time in the past and her aortic valve was severely affected. Her only hope was to have the valve replaced by a cardiac surgeon in Johannesburg, and it was in my power to arrange this, at Government expense.

Travelling from one place to another in the Republic was very difficult for '*Bantu*' people, so I created an elaborate travel pass on government notepaper, and stamped it portentously several times with every government rubber stamp I could find. There were several of these, some of which were extremely old, and I was very impressed with the result. I hoped the South African Police would be similarly impressed

The appointment was made, the pass did the trick, and in a few weeks she was home again with her new valve, feeling much better.

In her absence we employed a dreamy young woman called Mary to look after the house, to the delight of Templeton, the handsome and cheerful young gardener we had recently acquired.

We were very pleased when Elsie was able to resume her duties, as we had come to rely on her, and Peter loved her dearly.

CHAPTER 15
THE NEW CAESAR

Hurricane lamp

"As you know, a baby in utero that is lying across the mother's abdomen, cannot be delivered. Before the commencement of labour one would normally attempt to turn the foetus into a head down position by Bimanual External Version, in which having identified the head and back, gentle but firm pressure is applied simultaneously to the head and the breech, in order to turn it in the direction in which it is facing, and encouraging the head to descend into the pelvis. It is advantageous to elevate the head of the bed at the same time."

Professor Morris had come to all the way from England to little Basutoland to give us a lecture on Outmoded Obstetrical Techniques; that is to say ways of delivering babies that whilst outmoded in England, might still be valuable in the relatively primitive conditions that prevailed in this part of Africa. He was nearly right, and we were lucky that anyone was still around who knew about these things. We had been flown in from all parts of the territory to hear him, and we felt honoured and rather in awe. A real professor!

"If the foetus cannot be turned, or the mother is already in labour in a civilised country you would perform a Caesarean Section through the lower segment of the uterus, and this I propose to demonstrate later in the day, but if the facilities for this are not available, it would be necessary to perform Internal Podalic Version."

My God, would it?

"In this case the foetus' foot is grasped and drawn down though the cervix. If the membranes are still intact and the cervix is sufficiently dilated, the membranes can be ruptured, two fingers can be inserted and a foot grasped and drawn down through the cervix. The baby can then be delivered as a breech in the usual way."

H'm. The usual way, eh? When a baby is born feet first, with your palm uppermost, you place your forearm under the baby's belly with its arms and legs dangling either side. Then you put your middle finger in its mouth to bend its head forwards while you lift the legs straight up and back over the mother's abdomen with the other hand, while drawing it out. You have to be quick about it because the baby cannot breathe if its head is still inside and the umbilical cord is compressed between the baby's trunk and the mother's vagina. Once the baby's mouth appears there is time to relax a bit. I had done that successfully in the past, and once again the textbook was right, and it worked.

What's he saying now?

"Later in labour if no leg is immediately available the whole hand can be introduced, but there is considerable risk of rupturing the uterus."

Terrific. I think I'll give that one a miss.

"However, something has to be done, because a woman in obstructed labour will inevitably die if she cannot be delivered."

This all sounds a bit wild, even for Basutoland, where once Victor Ntsekhe, our psychiatrist, had to do a Caesar because he was the only doctor available at one of the out-stations.

After a thoughtful lunch, exchanging gossip about our various Districts, we were all asked to attend the operating theatre, where the worthy Professor, assisted by one of our own Medical Officers, Peter Witherow, would demonstrate a Lower Segment Caesarean Section.

"I understand that it is the custom here to perform a classical Caesarian Section. A simple enough procedure in all conscience, but one that leaves a significant risk of rupture of the scar in the uterus during subsequent labour."

He was absolutely right. We all did classical Caesars; that was all we knew how to do, though nobody had ever reported such a ruptured uterus to my knowledge. Anyway, let's see how they do it in a real hospital; if that's how we should describe the Queen Elizabeth II hospital in Maseru.

QE II was much better off than our little establishments. They had even got a real Boyle's anaesthetic machine, all shiny with chromium taps, bubbling jars of ether and trilene, a big cylinder of nitrous oxide and best of all, someone who knew how to use it. A great deal better than dropping ether onto a face mask, as at least you can be reasonably sure the patient will be asleep before you start. Once I had completely failed to anaesthetise a patient at Qacha's Nek. It seems that the altitude and a hot day had caused most of the ether to evaporate before the patient could inhale it. Also he had the reputation being a great drinker of *joala* and his liver may have learned the trick of disposing of noxious substances quickly. I gave up and sent him home still with his inguinal hernia.

The Professor is off again. Deftly wielding his scalpel, he continued:.

"We incise carefully across the lower abdomen so that we can expose the bladder without entering the peritoneal cavity. This reduces the risk of infection and adhesion of the peritoneum to the scar. The incision only needs to be about four inches long, below the Bikini line."

He was as good as his word. With Peter assisting he reflected the bladder downwards, exposing the lower segment, which is that part of the uterus which stretches rather than contracts as the baby descends through the birth canal. The lower segment was easy to see and rather thin as the patient was in labour and the baby's head well down. With gentle strokes of his scalpel he made an incision, extending it sideways with scissors. When the little head appeared; he grasped it firmly with both hands and drew it up and out, spluttering and sneezing, followed by the rest of the body, with its umbilical cord trailing back into the wound. Passing the baby to a nurse he cut the cord and reached back into the uterus to deliver the placenta. Finally he grasped the edges of the lower segment with broad bladed forceps to contain the bleeding, sewed the edges together, sewed up the abdomen, and it was all over.

We were very impressed, and vowed that we would do it that way in future. It had been a good day, and we enjoyed chatting with our fellow medics. It was a rare pleasure to meet our colleagues and compare notes, and reassuring to find out that we all had the same problems. However we all had to be back in our districts the same evening, so we said our farewells and set off home soon after the session was over.

Clouds were beginning to pile up as we droned back through the mountain peaks to Qacha's Nek.

"Can't hang about", said Tony Clegg, who was flying me that evening, as we landed. "Got to get back before the weather breaks."

I jumped out and he roared up the strip, turned the plane round and was off down again in a cloud of dust. I watched him go and he was soon out of sight. I looked at the gathering clouds. We desperately needed the rain to bring on some new grazing for the skinny cattle, and maybe some was on its way at last.

"How was Maseru?" asked Celia over supper.

"Not as nice as here. This chap Morris said we were doing Caesars all wrong and showed us the proper way."

"Will it work here?"

Tri-pacer at Maseru

"Think so. We've got all the instruments we need. Mind you it's a bit more scary than the good old classical Caesar."

That night there was a stupendous thunderstorm. Celia and I spent much of the night admiring the lightning as it danced and flickered round the mountains. The thunder was continuous. What an incredible display of energy! There was one tremendous flash and almost simultaneous explosion that left us dazed, and then the storm grumbled off. I ventured out onto the *stoep*, but by now the rain was so heavy that there was nothing to be seen, so we went back to bed.

The storm cleared the air and the next day sun was back in position, pouring light onto the newly washed landscape. Everything smelt wonderfully fresh.

After our morning bath together we breakfasted on the veranda, to the cooing of doves and the sweet smell of burning cow dung. All was well with the world.

Until that evening. Though the diesel generator started all right, it just whizzed round without making any electricity, and hurricane lamps had to be found, lit and hung around the hospital as well as at home. Strange, as the generator was always so reliable.

The next day I phoned the DMS in Maseru to ask what to do. Phoning anyone outside the district was always exciting. I enjoyed using the beautiful old Swedish handset with its horn mouthpiece, which sat so demurely on its cradle above a metal box which was painted black and decorated with gold foliage. I twirled the handle, and listened as the various exchanges connected up. I was careful not to touch the handle until the end of the conversation, as turning it means that the call is over, and all the operators saw it is the signal to pull out their plugs. If you turned it by mistake, your conversation would come to an abrupt end, as I had found to my cost on a previous occasion.

"Get an engineer up from Matatiele," advised the DMS..

The engineer couldn't make it until the following day, and as it happened a woman in obstructed labour was admitted at midday on the same day. She was exhausted and clearly I would have to do a Caesar as soon as possible, and now I knew how to do one properly.

The snag was that we had no electricity and therefore no spotlight in the theatre. However, sunlight was pouring through the glass roof and illuminating everything with great clarity, so I decided to go ahead and perform my first Lower Segment Caesar anyway.

I put up a saline drip to be on the safe side. The patient was soon asleep, with Butler holding up her chin and the Schimmelbusch mask with his left hand, and dripping the ether judiciously with his right hand.

I scrubbed up, and masked, gowned and gloved made the first incision, a replica of that made by the worthy Professor. So far so good. I incised the lower segment and the baby's head appeared. I delivered it and out came the rest of the baby; I clamped and cut the cord, passed baby to nurse, and delivered the placenta. There, that wasn't too difficult, was it?

"Ergometrine, please." Nurse gave the injection into the mother's thigh. Now for the lips of the incision in the uterus. There was a fair amount of blood, but that couldn't be the only reason why it was so difficult to make out what was what.

The reason was that it was getting darker and darker. A cloud had come up from somewhere out of the clear blue sky and blotted out the sun, and soon we were groping about in premature twilight. As I couldn't see anything I had to feel for the lips of the incision in the lower segment with my fingertips. I managed to apply the forceps, drew up the lips up and held out my hand for the large curved needle with strong gut through the eye, that Florry had prepared.

"I think I'll do a continuous suture, though the Professor recommended separate stitches. Then at least we will know the edges can't bleed, and it'll be quicker." I was sweating a bit by then. I was dimly aware of the baby spluttering somewhere as it was sucked out.

"Let's clear some of this blood away so that I can make out how things are. Could somebody mop my forehead before I start dripping into the wound?" Florry mopped away in the patient with gauze swabs and somebody else mopped my forehead. I felt around in the wound. There was no more bleeding and the uterus was nicely contracted, so I covered the continuous suture by tacking the bladder back in position and sewed up her abdomen.

I straightened my creaking back "How is she, Butler?"

"She's fine, doctor. Pulse strong and steady. She'll soon be round.."

* * *

Later that day the engineer arrived. The sun was shining again by now.

"The trouble is she's got no magnetism in her field coils, " he said in his warm South African accent. The engine was chugging away.

"What does that mean?" I enquired.

"You see the generator there, on the left of the engine? Well it has electromagnets in it, and the armature rotating in the magnetic field makes the electricity, or it should do."

"So what's the problem?"

"If you don't have a bit of permanent magnetism in the core of the electromagnets, you can't make any electricity at all. When things are working properly, the armature rotating in this residual magnetic field makes just enough electricity for the coils to energise the electromagnets properly, and then they can make the real thing. But something has wiped the magnets clean, so no electricity is coming out. A lightning strike to the transmission line between here and the hospital, maybe?"

So that's what that crash of thunder meant! He attached a car battery to the salient contacts to introduce a little magnetism into the coils, and immediately the engine note slowed and deepened as the generator took the load.

"She'll be all right now, as the poles will stay magnetised." He unclipped the battery leads. " Let me know if you have any more problems.".

Off he bustled to his pickup, carrying the battery in both hands and with his tool bag slung over his shoulder. He leapt in, started up and with a farewell wave crunched off down the gravel road at high speed.

As I trudged back to the house I mused over the previous afternoon. Finishing off an operation by touch had been an alarming experience, but there hadn't been much choice. It would have been much simpler if I had done a good, old fashioned Classical Caesar, whatever the supposed hazards to the mother in subsequent labours. In fact the mother recovered without a hitch, but I wasn't at all sure which operation I would do the next time.

As it happens there was no next time while I was at Qacha's Nek. That was the last one I did there, though I managed a few more Lower Segment Caesars successfully in Maseru, even two in one day, which brought my total to thirteen.

CHAPTER 16
KISS OF LIFE?

Sulphur ointment is good for scabies

"Listen to this," I said to Celia one morning when we were opening our mail. Letters and magazines are a welcome reminder that there is a world still turning somewhere else when you are far from home, and that family and friends are busy living their lives elsewhere.

"It's a circular from some outfit in Bombay asking me to send for one of their sex pills. I quote: *the pill should be held in the cheek while performing the sexual act and performance will be immeasurably enhanced. Since it does not alter it may be retrieved if accidentally swallowed.* What do you think about that?"

"I think it's quite revolting."

"There's more. It comes in two styles, silver and gold. The gold one costs more but works even better. How about it? It's only a fiver"

"Don't be silly."

There was an intriguing packet which I was saving until last. It came from America. I remembered that six weeks before I had replied to an advertisement by a high powered electronics firm in the *Scientific American* which said "Send for one of our revolutionary new binary decisionometers. Absolutely free." There was something pleasingly ironic about sitting in our mountain eyrie, reading about the latest scientific discoveries.

I slit open the packet to reveal a slim blue box with "Binary Decisionometer" inscribed on it in gold. Just what I needed, several times a day. What electronic device could there be in so small a box? It must be incredibly sophisticated. I opened the box and was stunned to see a large golden coin. On one side it said: *Do it!* and on the other: *The hell with it!*

Ah well.

"Do you want to hear the good news?" I said, turning the coin over in my hand.

"What's that?" Celia replied.

"The twenty dozen toilet rolls have arrived at last! The situation is saved. It's only taken about three months. I haven't dared ask how they have managed in the meanwhile."

* * *

Soon after our wedding I had bought a car, the first one I had ever owned. It was a brand new Opel Kapitan estate; it was blue with a white roof and I was very proud of it. In fact it was not really man enough for Basutoland's roads, or lack of roads, and the tops of the front wheels leaned towards each other more and more as the weeks passed. This problem was finally solved in a garage down in South Africa.

"Don't worry, man," said the mechanic as he jacked up the front of the car, "this is always happening."

In no time he had removed the front wheels and the entire front axle unit. He placed a hydraulic ram between the two uprights and pumped it up until he had forced them straight again. He produced a metal plate, put on his goggles, lit up his oxy-acetylene burner and welded it on to the back of the cross member. When it had cooled he slapped on some quick-drying paint and re-assembled the car.

"It won't happen again," he assured me; and he was right.

Which was just as well, because a few days later there was a phone call from Tars Francis' trading store at Whitehill, some miles away along the valley on the road to Sekake's. There was a woman having difficulty delivering a baby nearby, and could we come as soon as possible? I hijacked a midwife from the labour ward, and set off in the Opel.

The Orange River generally runs between steep slopes, but at one place there is a small flat plain on a spur of land where the river makes a tight curve. When we arrived at this place, there was a cluster of women with their backs to me and a disconsolate looking man sitting on a rock some distance away. Every now and then the man would get up and lurch towards the women, who would chase him back to his rock, shouting and waving sticks.

"Who is that man who seems to be upsetting them?" I asked the midwife who had grabbed her bag and joined me when we received the phone call.

"Oh, I expect that will be the father of the baby", she replied with a laugh, "delivering babies is women's work in this country; and men have to keep well out of the way."

The cluster separated as we approached to reveal a young woman lying on the ground, evidently in the final stages of labour. Many hands lifted her into the back of the estate car just in time for the final push that brought the baby into the world. It was only five pounds or so but seemed lusty enough. So when the cord and placenta had been dealt with I handed the little mite to his mother and we bumped along the dirt road back to the hospital, about forty minutes away. A little girl.

It wasn't until we had her settled in our brand new maternity ward, that it was possible to examine her properly, where I found that labour wasn't over; the baby in her arms was the first of twins and that there was another baby to come. Sewing up the tears in her perineum would have to wait.

"Why do they push so hard that they exhaust themselves and end up with these awful tears?" I asked the midwife.

"Because there is a belief that if the baby does not appear in twenty four hours the husband is not the father," she replied.

"But there is no point in pushing until the cervix is fully dilated, it won't hurry things along at all."

"We tell them this over and over again but they will not listen. There are many customs here which are hard to change, and childbirth is always supervised by the old women of the village. Perhaps you should tell them, maybe they would listen to you."

"I'll think about it." It would be interesting to meet some traditional midwives on their own territory.

We laid our hands on her abdomen. Contractions had been very feeble, but they seemed to be strengthening. We took it in turns to listen with the monaural stethoscope. We could just hear the little heartbeat ticking away against the slower rushing of its mother's circulation.

In due course the second twin arrived. It was a little boy, less than five pounds in weight, and he made no attempt to breathe. The midwife sucked him out, we patted his feet, but still he wouldn't breathe. I listened to his heart, and timed the rate. It was beating at about 90 to the minute, and the rate was beginning to fall even as I listened. We tried tilting him to and fro in the hope that his moving guts would help to inflate his lungs, but he still wouldn't breathe. His pulse rate fell still further, and his lips began to go blue.

"I'm going to have to try a bit of mouth to mouth," I said, laying him on a table with his head to my right and my left hand resting on his upper abdomen and placing my lips over his mouth and nose.

Gently I tilted his head back and puffed cheekfuls of air into him. It was with great relief that I saw out of the corner of my eye that his chest was rising and falling with each puff. After a while I straightened up and reached for the stethoscope so that I could listen to his heart. It was beating at the rate of 110 to the minute; clearly he was getting the required oxygen, but he still made no attempt to breathe for himself, and his heart rate began to fall again, so I breathed for him again.

I found that despite my care his stomach was inflating, but if I massaged his upper abdomen gently, he brought up the air in burps. Clearly this was going to take a while, so I asked for a chair, and re-arranged him so that I could carry on in more comfort.

* * *

It took seven hours before his heart rate finally ceased to respond. Each time I paused his heart beat more and more slowly, and in the end I could not restore it at all. I would have stopped sooner, but his heart speeded up every time I breathed for him, so that there was no particular time at which I felt I could give up. It was terribly disappointing. The whole exhausting exercise had been a complete waste of time. It was quite useless. He died anyway. Perhaps it would have been kinder to his mother to have let him go in the first place.

"Don't worry, you did your best," said Celia when I finally came home to bed. But I did worry. I had held that fragile little life in my hands all that time and had been unable to stop it slipping away. Surely there was more that could have been done.

The first baby had emerged between her mother's vagina and her rectum, so there was some complicated reconstruction to be performed the next morning. The young woman made no complaint about the death of the second twin, happy that at least one of them had survived. A baby dying was so common in Basutoland in those days, that nobody made much fuss about it.

Florry and her colleagues had kept a two pound premature baby

119

alive for three weeks in a shoe box, by oiling it, wrapping it in cotton wool and feeding it with expressed breast milk through a pipette. Just when they thought they had won, it quite suddenly died.

Alternation of delight and despair at what I was achieving, or failing to achieve, gradually wore me down over the days and weeks. Despite the wonderful setting and splendid people, after two years my time was running out, and I was beginning to feel that I was more of a liability than an asset. If anyone was seriously thinking of making a career of this kind of work, they should have much more training than I had had, and should serve a lengthy apprenticeship under supervision.

So the time to return to Maseru was rapidly approaching. I was to finish my contract helping out here and there for our last few weeks.

"As you will be leaving soon, we are holding a party for you and Mrs Smith down by the Sejabatho River next Wednesday evening," said Butler Panyane one day.

Basuto parties are notable for wonderful speech making. I had been to one in the village hall near the camp, where, after we had sung Haydn's *Creation* to the tonic sol-fa, I was expected make several speeches. After the first one, which wasn't up to much, I could think of nothing more to say. In contrast to my feeble efforts, the other speech makers seemed to be able to go on for ages, with remarkable eloquence and fine gestures. I was afraid that this would happen again, but my reputation as an orator must have preceded me, as I was only required to proclaim a toast.

The joala arrives for the party

120

It was a memorable party indeed.

A pile of wood had been gathered and set on fire on the slope above the river. When it was settling down after a fine blaze, a sheet of corrugated iron was thrown over it. A sheep was killed and dismembered, and the meat thrown onto the corrugated iron to roast.

As the sun began to set behind the mountains half a dozen lissom young women appeared over the hill with gallon cans of *joala* (fermented millet beer) on their heads.

The first can was passed to me, so I hoisted it to my lips and took a deep draught of the thin, fizzy porridge. "*Khotso! Pula! Nala!*.....Peace! Rain! Prosperity!" I cried. and "*Khotso, Pula, Nala!*" they replied. I passed the can to my neighbour, and so the loving cup went round.

How is it that people who have so little can make so much delight?

All too soon, and with great sadness when it came to the point, we drove round to camp to say our goodbyes to black and white friends alike. The hospital staff assembled and Mr. Christmas, the gaoler, presented us with a set of four red striped containers, for tea, coffee, sugar and flour, labelled in English and *Afrikaans*.

We hadn't anticipated the extent to which these good people had wound themselves into our hearts.

CHAPTER 17
BACK TO MASERU

Mounted policeman

After a last look at our first home and the wonderful mountains that surrounded it, we piled our stuff into the Opel and drove down the track out of Basutoland to Mataiele and turned south round the mountains. It was a pretty awful dirt road, though probably not much more awful than most. At one point there were a series of ridges, gradual at one side and steep at the other. The road went straight up the gradual side, so I was tempted to speed up and rumble over the corrugations instead of banging into each ridge as it came; but when I reached the skyline, the road suddenly changed direction at a sharp angle to go down the steep side. After nearly flying off into oblivion a couple of times, I got the hang of it.

The terrain was stony desert, buff coloured and shaley, with small, sparse bushes here and there. Even the ubiquitous herdboys were nowhere to be seen. You wonder how anything survives in such an arid place.

As usual I became very sleepy in the afternoon, and Celia drove while I dozed with Peter on my knee. Awakened by a thumping sound, we found that it was Peter's head bouncing off the door as we negotiated the potholes, but he didn't wake up, so presumably he was coming to no harm. I shifted him over and went back to sleep again.

It would be a great mistake to break down on that winding mountainous track. Though there was one petrol station, between Matatiele and Mohale's Hoek, there was a seventy mile gap either side of it, and as there was no traffic, nor any houses or phones, there was little chance of being rescued for many hours if one was in trouble.

We re-entered Basutoland through the south eastern border gate near Mohale's Hoek, and drove through Mafateng, and finally the last thirty miles north to Maseru. We drove around for some time and eventually located our new home, a modern bungalow in a row of identical modern bungalows on the outskirts of the little town.

The outlook from the front door was extremely boring compared with what we were used to. On the other side of the dirt road was a wire fence which led onto a dry, flat field with scattered wisps of dry grass growing here and there. The mountains were far away now, blue and tiny in the distance.

There was no choice but to make the best of it. We had a little garden with a patch of dusty lawn and rows of nectarines. We strung a series of tin cans with pebbles inside amongst them in such a way that a little boy could rattle them by yanking the end of the string all day to frighten the birds away for a *tickey*. This was the name given originally to a silver threepenny bit, but though these had been superseded by the new coinage, it was still applied to the smallest silver coin. When we had settled in we redecorated the inside of the house, painting the walls different colours and the bedroom ceiling yellow as was the fashion at the time.

Peter, who was approaching his second birthday, seemed to like his new home. Celia shocked the locals by allowing him to go round without shoes, just in a sun hat and light clothes, when he wasn't stark naked. We were a bit baffled by this disapproval; maybe they were appalled because we might be going native, and it was perceived as important to maintain standards. We were apparently letting the side down rather badly. It seemed to us that most white babies we came across were ridiculously overdressed.

I would wrap up well in the frosty mornings and drive off the to the Queen Elizabeth II hospital. We were happy enough and people were very friendly, but we had been spoiled, and missed the freedom and eccentricity of Qacha's Nek. In the capital, though it was scarcely bigger than a medium sized English village, it was necessary to behave properly. After all, it was the capital and the Resident Commissioner, who was the

Queen's representative, and all government offices were located here. Celia was taken round to call on the senior wives, wearing a hat and gloves, and we had to sign the book at the Residency. We could not see the point of all this palaver, until it was explained that it meant we would be invited to parties and other Government happenings. I was asked once again to sign the Official Secrets Act and the Oath of Allegiance to the Queen.

For the third time I told them that whilst I wanted to swear allegiance to the Queen, I wouldn't sign the Official Secrets Act as it said silly things. For example I would have to swear never to destroy any Government correspondence, when there was nowhere to put the piles of paper that built up.

I went to see Stephen Howard, now the District Commissioner for Maseru, to complain. When I arrived I was directed to his *rondavel*, where he was printing large black and white photographs in buckets of chemical, as there was no running water. After clattering about for a while he let me in, pulled the door to and switched on the red light. "Nobody pays any attention to that," he said as he looked closely at an emerging print, grunted his satisfaction, dipped it in the wash bucket and dropped it in the fixer, "We burned a pile of papers in a huge bonfire behind my office only a couple of weeks ago. We had to as there was no room for the new stuff."

"Well then, you shouldn't have signed the Act either if you weren't going to stick to it," I said. "Can't I just swear the Oath of Allegiance to the Queen? I really want to do that." He looked at me pityingly. "It's not much to ask, you only have to make a swear and sign a couple of bits of paper. Anyone who works for the government has to." He fished out the print and dropped it into the final bucket of water.

I thought about this as I strolled back to the bungalow. It seemed there was no way out. You either swore both or neither. They could scarcely refuse to give me the job, as my time in Basutoland was almost over. In the end I never signed either of them.

Queen Elizabeth II hospital was bigger than mine at Qacha's Nek, with perhaps a couple of hundred beds, and it was much better equipped. What we actually did was similar; and though we were busy, as there were several of us, I had regular time off. We were operating or doing rounds of the wards most of the day and there was a dispensary seething with patients next to the hospital which we tried to avoid, in the hope that someone else was seeing to the patients. This was rarely the case, and from time to time a nurse would drag one of us across, usually when we were having a coffee break.

It was winter, and the temperature throughout the day fluctuated wildly. It was bitterly cold at first, but after a morning's work I was so hot that I would peel off my jersey. As it was still warm at the end of the day, I would leave it behind at the hospital so that I had nothing to wrap up in the following morning.

There had been some changes since we were last there. David Standing had moved on from being a senior medical officer to be Director of Medical Services in Bechuanaland, which was a great shame, as he was a very experienced surgeon and liked to teach. Fortunately we still had the delightful Aaron D. ('Adie') Lebona, who had been trained at the University of Witwatersrand before the South African government forbade them to take *Bantu* students. With Dr Jacques, who had been working in Maseru for some years, and me, that made four. We did what we could, both medically and surgically, with varying success.

Victor Ntsekhe, another witty and delightful Mosuto, was our psychiatrist, and he had trained at the Maudsley Hospital in London. He had a ward full of patients who all seemed quite mad. Some were curled up into small balls, some were declaiming at length, some scribbling furiously on page after page.

"What on earth is going on here, Victor?" I asked him.

"They are abreacting on LSD. I learned how to do this when I was on a course at the Maudsley. It's a sort of blanket therapy for neurotic illnesses that won't respond to anything else. It looks a bit chaotic at the moment because they are all hallucinating, but at six o'clock they all have an injection of Largactil, and that settles them down. It seems to be quite effective."

To my surprise this bizarre therapy seemed to do some good. Certainly it cured a policeman from Qacha's Nek who suffered from blindness whenever he was asked to fill in a form. He decided to get better, though whether it was the LSD that brought this about was not clear.

As this was Basutoland, Victor doubled up as neurosurgeon for head injuries. He reckoned that you could not remove good brain with the sucker, only the mashed bits, so he would cheerfully suck out anything loose, then tidy things up. On one occasion when visiting some disturbed patients in Butha-Buthe, he had to perform an emergency Caesarean section for an obstructed labour, because the regular Medical Officer was out of camp. Apparently everybody survived.

There was one other doctor, who had trained in Switzerland, but he only had a basic medical, and not surgical, qualification. This meant that he was not allowed to operate, but he could give a useful anaesthetic with the Boyle's machine, using real nitrous oxide gas. He was also doing a tuberculosis survey for the World Health Organisation, which irritated us a bit as he was much better paid than we were, despite doing no surgery.

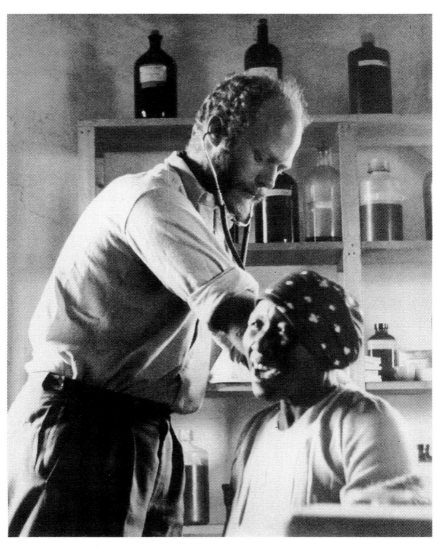

Cold stethoscope at Simonkong

For a while we had a fully trained surgeon called Trevor Loutit, but he disappeared quite soon and we were left to our own devices again. Sometimes these devices worked, sometimes they didn't. Since we had had no special training, it was difficult to know what you could or could not do. I had one man who had broken one of his femurs some time before, and the lower end was rammed right up against his pelvis, shortening his leg by several inches, but in spite of this he could walk, after a fashion. Thinking I could improve on this I managed to lever his femur back into alignment and fasten it by screwing a plate across the fracture, but the massive muscles of his thigh were too much for it, and the plate bent to such an angle that he couldn't use his leg at all. We sent him to Bloemfontein to see a real Orthopaedic surgeon, but it would have been better either to have sent him there in the first place, or to have left it alone.

Some things worked really well. A policeman had dislocated his hip playing football and the clunk as it jumped back into place when I put his leg over my shoulder and lifted his unconscious body off the table, was deeply satisfying.

We had to run a weekly dispensary up in the mountains at Simonkong. When it was dry the pilot had to zoom up and down until all the sheep had scattered off the airstrip; but when it had been raining for a while, the strip was awash, and the planes landed and took off with a huge fountain of spray cascading over the wings. There was a hill at the end of the runway, so that the pilot had to pull up to avoid it, turn left before he stalled and swoop down the winding Maletsanyane gorge to pick up flying speed. It was thrilling watching the rocky walls of the gorge streak past, apparently almost touching the wingtips, until the little plane was going fast enough to climb out.

There is a waterfall about a thousand feet high pouring over the edge of the gorge, which makes it the highest in Southern Africa. It is only a few feet wide so the water plunges down like a bridal veil. On one occasion I had a roll in the ice-fringed stream right on the edge of the ravine, and later sat on the verge and watched the sheep at the bottom; which looked like maggots at such a distance. It was one of those places where you think it would be nice to jump off and float away. Celia came with me once, and we had a lovely conversation with a herd boy, by scratching pictures on his brown forearm with a twig.

On one of these outings an exhausted young man with a camera turned up. His name was Karl de Haan and he came from Holland. He had been riding round the mountains taking photos until his horse wore out, then walked till his feet wore out. The dispensary at Simonkong was of the customary design. A dispenser and I saw patients in a little *rondavel*, with a table, two chairs and a shelf of bottles. Karl took some photographs there while I was busy, and as there was a spare seat in the plane, we gave him a lift back, and he stayed with us for a few days.

We had nothing to do one evening so I took him out onto the veldt with a handful of assegais I had acquired, and showed him how to throw them. I demonstrated how it was done. "You hold it like this?" he asked, "and throw it like this?" I said that it looked as if he had got the idea. He then threw the spear so far that it flew practically out of sight. It turned out that he was a reserve Olympic javelin thrower for Holland so I felt extremely stupid. After he had gone home he sent us some beautiful photographs he had taken in Simonkong, and some in the Queen Elizabeth hospital.

These were uncertain times. The little country was being progressively handed over to the Basuto, and there was some violent jockeying for power, particularly between the Chieftainship and the Congress parties, and some sort of civil disturbance seemed to be quite possible.

We made great friends with Chris and Jackie Willoughby. He was an officer in the Special Branch and I used to tease him by making up revolutionary scenarios and asking him what he would do about them. One evening, over a beer, I wheedled the police radio frequency out of him and a few days later told him that I had set up a jammer on the hill while I was abducting a terrorist from the hospital via a culvert. I was delighted to see the hospital was crawling with Basuto policemen the next day.

Schoolboy stuff, but fun.

Soon Jackie produced the longest baby we had ever seen, called Rupert. He cried a lot, and after I had made a brilliant diagnosis of chronic hunger, he was fed on demand and quietened down.

One evening Chris rushed in with a crumpled fag packet on which was scribbled "We are having a party for the C-in-C South Atlantic. Do come" in the hand of the Resident Commissioner's wife. "You can take this as gilt-edged" said Chris, earnestly.

Quite a party it was. I remember meeting the Admiral and then getting involved with some sprightly young Agricultural Officers who were limbo dancing in a large room with a wooden floor. I tried to dance under the stick, which was only a couple of feet above the floor, but fell backwards and was dragged bodily out of the way by one fellow on each leg, whereupon a large sliver of wood stuck firmly into my back, and I had to be taken to the hospital to have it removed.

At a similar party I felt moved to mount a gorgeous big black horse with a cropped, stand-up mane, like a horse in a Greek sculpture, that was grazing outside the French windows and ride him bareback round the paddock in my dinner jacket suit and black bow tie. I hoped I was a stirring sight. The owner was furious and demanded that I dismount, so I did so with as much dignity as I could muster. That beautiful horse died later of ragwort poisoning.

One party we threw in our little bungalow ended up with people trying to tie each other up with ropes so that they couldn't escape. We found that it was impossible to do this. Somebody even wriggled out of having his thumbs tied to his bootlaces behind his back.

There were many more European children around than we were used to, and one day John Plyman, the Education Officer, organised a paper chase on horseback to entertain them. The terrain around Maseru was pretty flat; there were barbed wire fences and several *dongas*, where the rain had washed deep gullies through the loose, sandy soil. I borrowed a real Basuto pony so that I could join in. We were a motley crew, adults and children, horses of all sizes and shapes, charging over the countryside. My little pony seemed to be able to fly in sheer joy, his little hooves barely touching the ground, and when he came to a *donga* scuttled down one side, danced among the boulders and up the other side before I knew what was happening. The children always seemed to arrive at the stops before me, but then their horses were generally bigger.

One day Celia borrowed a big horse and I the pony, and we rode up to the race track a mile or two out of town, which was deserted at the time. After a while Celia set off for the finishing post with me trundling behind in a shower of clods. Fired with excitement I urged the little beast to maximum effort and gradually pounded past Celia and her steed, crossing the line a fraction of a second before her. Flushed with triumph I crowed that I had won. "Oh, was it a race, then?" said Celia disdainfully. I was crestfallen.

Basuto patients were extremely amenable, possibly because of the culture gap, but European patients were rather more difficult. One senior police officer described how a weight pressed on his head as he climbed the stairs to his office, so heavy that he could barely get to the top. He told me about the problems he was having to deal with, which included an assassination attempt on a senior Basuto politician.

"It looks to me as if you are suffering from the stresses of your job, and should have some time off." I suggested.

"No can do, I'm afraid. As it happens I am absolutely essential. You'll have to give me something to keep me going," so I put him on anti-depressant medication and hoped for the best.

My essays into private medicine were a failure. I took one white boy's appendix out, (the Basuto hardly ever had appendicitis or peptic ulcers, thank God) and when I sent his father a bill, not only did he refuse to pay it, he publicly abused me in the street, though the boy had recovered without incident. I had no idea how to deal with this irrational hostility, so I let him be and vowed never to take on a private patient again.

People came and went much more that they did at Qacha's Nek, and some of them were distinctly odd. I was called to the hotel one day to find a scrawny little man called Fisher in bed, who told me that he had abdominal pain. He also told me that he was the *Daily Telegraph* correspondent for Southern Africa, that he had a silver plate in his head, and that he was the grandson of Admiral Fisher, the great British Admiral of the first world war. He went on to describe the Admiral's ancestral home in Britain, with family portraits on the wall, where he used to visit his grandparents. He also assured me that it was his grandmother who was the real power behind the old boy.

He spoke at length in great detail about his life. I was quite entranced, but found it all a bit hard to believe, and mentioned it to Chris Willoughby. He told me later that the man's real name was Visser and he was a pathological liar, was wanted by the South African Police, and was found later hiding in the boot of a car.

What a pity!

Though Basutoland was only a poor little country the size of Yorkshire, being surrounded by the increasingly isolated and fascist Republic of South Africa, it had a political significance out of all proportion to its size.

I was visited in surgery by an American airforce pilot with a hangover, who had just flown in a senior diplomat in quite a large plane. "Have you ever tried driving an airplane with a hangover, Doc?" I had to admit that I had never had the opportunity.

Politicians were always popping in and out. One fellow turned up alleging that he was Winston Churchill. "Really?" said one of our young government officials, "in that case I'm Joe Stalin." It emerged that it really was Winston Churchill, MP, grandson of the war time leader.

After church on Sunday mornings we would often repair to the Maseru Club for a beer and if it was warm, a swim. The Club had originally been set up for white people only, but they could not keep out Adie Lebona, with his charming ways and single figure golf handicap. There was a nine hole golf course, as well as the swimming pool, tennis courts and bar.

Tobias and the Angel, the play by J.M.Barrie based on the story of Tobit in the Apocrypha, was chosen for the Club's Christmas entertainment. John Plyman, who was short, fat and Puckish, played Tobias; Celia played Sarah, and I the archangel Raphael. The little hall had a tin roof which magnified the noise of the rain and occasional hailstorms made such a racket that sometimes we couldn't hear anything at all, which made rehearsing difficult. When the great day came and curtain eventually went up to a packed house, there was spontaneous applause for the set. Someone had created the silhouette of a little desert oasis town, behind which dawn gradually rose.

Stephen Howard, one time our District Commissioner for Qacha's Nek, was the producer. He was quite happy with Celia's acting skills, but he found me more difficult. He told me to speak as if down a long tube, which is apparently how angels speak. In the write-up for the local paper the critic said: "Colin Smith would have been quite good as the Archangel Raphael if he had not sounded as if he was speaking down a tube," which was rather galling.

I was supposed to disappear in a flash at the very end of the play, so we had arranged for someone to discharge the flash from his camera at the appropriate time. Unfortunately the chap who was supposed to do it, having nothing else to do all through the play, was tippling at a whisky bottle and when the time came he was so drunk that he couldn't make the camera obey his commands, and the flash went off under the stage some time later.

Despite this, the play was great fun and was well received.

CHAPTER 18
A VERY TOUGH YOUNG WOMAN

A terrible weapon

Autumn had passed and first chill breezes of winter began to swirl round the Queen Elizabeth II hospital as the days shortened, so that it looked like an illuminated ferryboat marooned in its dusty compound opposite Barclay's bank.

As time went by we realised that Maseru had changed quite a lot since I arrived, two and a half years before. There was an uneasiness in the air. A Basuto politician had found a bomb under his car, the Republic of South Africa was making belligerent noises, and had even sent in a posse of soldiers to try and take out a dissident called Ganyile who had taken shelter in the mountains in Qacha's Nek. While he was there we invited him to tea and he seemed a perfectly reasonable fellow. Control was being handed over to the Basuto bit by bit as independence approached, and this seemed to breed a number of people prepared to take up arms to get their hands on political power. I had bought a rather rickety 7mm Browning automatic pistol for £7 from Brian Lee, the Police Superintendent at Qacha's Nek, and I kept it on top of the bedroom wardrobe in case there was civil unrest and someone broke in.

I was uneasy about this, as it seemed to conflict with Jesus' teaching about turning the other cheek, but I felt that since I would have no hesitation in trying to kill anyone who threatened Celia and little Peter, even if I only had a teapot as a weapon, that I might as well have a proper gun with which to do it. I had asked the Catholic priest at Eagle's Peak mission station near Qacha's Nek, if it was all right for a Christian to possess a gun and the priest had said it was justified under certain circumstances, and that you could shoot somebody in defence of your family, so I felt a bit better about it.

Getting a licence was quite straightforward; I simply went to the police station and asked for one, and a flimsy form, to the effect that I was the legitimate owner of the gun in question, was made out then and there, with a carbon copy for records.

"No, my children play with them. I leave them lying about the house so that they get used to them" Brian Lee had said when I asked him about security, "then they get to know how dangerous they are. It's the people who are not used to them who get into trouble. I train them myself and they show firearms proper respect."

However I was still afraid of shooting someone by mistake, possibly myself, so kept the pistol on top of the bedroom wardrobe with the safety catch on, no round in the chamber, and the magazine not pushed home into the grip. All of this meant that if we had really been in danger from an intruder, by the time I had fetched the pistol from the top of the wardrobe and made it ready, an assassin could have shot everybody twice over.

Ammunition could be bought at a hardware store in the Republic on production of the licence. It was an amazingly simple business compared with the strict rules back home in Great Britain. I found it extremely difficult to shoot with any precision. Chris Willoughby had a smart automatic pistol, a 9mm Beretta I think it was, and I took my rickety Browning, and off we went shooting at beer cans in a suitably secluded bit of countryside up near the race course.

It was then that the scales fell from my eyes. Chris, who gave the impression of being a slightly simple but tall, handsome and extremely well bred gentleman, was in fact a crack shot. It is a mistake to underestimate such men. Beer can after beer can flew away when he was shooting, while mine remained stubbornly in place. I began to treat the Special Branch, which I had previously seen as a bit of a joke, with more respect.

Not too much though. I tried to barge into the room at the back of his office where the secret files were kept, to see if they had a dossier on me, but was barged back again by a buxom young woman. So I crept round to a side window and popped up and said "Up with Mao Tse Tung!" at the top of my voice and then ran off. Mao was the pet hate figure at the time.

One morning as I swung the blue Opel into the hospital car park, my mind was full of all sorts of thing; Celia and the baby at the bungalow, the political problems in the territory, memories of the mountain hospital at Qacha's Nek, glad and sorry at the same time to be nearer the centre of things, happy to have some colleagues to share the anxieties, yet missing the extraordinary freedom of the mountains. I was still preoccupied as I pulled up, and walked across the sand into the side door of the hospital.

I sauntered down the corridor to the little rest room where the MOs would sit and drink coffee - often still in their bloodstained white gowns - either discussing the most recent operations and other happenings around the hospital, or merely gossiping about local affairs.

A Basuto nurse put her head round the door: "They have just brought in a woman in with head wounds, could somebody come?"

"Your turn Colin, I'm off home," said one of my colleagues, pulling off his gown and throwing it into the bin in the corner of the rest room.

Swallowing the now familiar hint of panic, I grabbed a white coat and followed the nurse to the reception area. Seated there was a young Basuto woman, her blanket pinned over her shoulders, and some bloodstained rags round her head and part of her face. There were a number of similarly blanketed men standing about silently. One of them stepped forward.

"*Morena ngaka*," he said, his warm voice betrayed by the anxiety furrowing his brow. Even after two years on my own in Qacha's Nek I still felt unworthy when addressed as doctor in Sesuto, let alone chief and doctor. "This young woman is my daughter. She has been hit many times on the head by a bad man. So I brought her here on the back of my lorry."

"Quite right. How long did it take?"

"It was far from here. Fifteen hours."

I was relieved. Anyone who could survive fifteen hours on the back of a lorry could not be badly hurt. Taking her hand, I led her into the side room where she climbed onto the operating table without saying a word. I unwound the rags.

It was an appalling sight. There were four clefts in her head. The worst had entered her left brow, passed through her eye and penetrated to the base of her nose. Her brain, grey and glistening in the theatre lights, was visible in the bottom of the cleft, as it was in two of the other wounds which had been cut at intervals across her skull. The cleft into her right brow was superficial, merely exposing her skull.

"How did this happen?" I asked.

"Her man was angry with her and hit her with his axe," was the simple reply.

Where to start? As I inspected these terrible wounds I marvelled at her incredible composure. She was in so little distress. A European would surely have died on principle after wounds like that. She was simply lying there, patiently, waiting for whatever was going to happen next. At least there did not seem to be any need for resuscitation. There was little overt bleeding, so maybe it would be enough just to tidy things up under local anaesthetic and hope for the best.

The nurse brought up a tray of mercurochrome disinfectant, various sterile sutures and needles, and a syringe. I scrubbed up and a put on the gown which was handed to me with sterile tongs, and snapped on rubber gloves. Holding the gauze swabs in a pair of long forceps, I carefully cleaned around the wounds. Her short tightly curled black hair would make suturing difficult.

"Would you shave round the wounds, please nurse, being very careful that none of the hair falls in."

When she had been shaved, a nurse swabbed the rubber stopper of the vial of Lignocaine and presented it so that I could pierce it with the syringe and draw up 10 ccs of the local anaesthetic. I had chosen a syringe with a bayonet lock for the needle, so that it could not fly off if I had to apply pressure to the plunger, to force the anaesthetic into the tough places of her scalp.

Apart from a few fragments of some unidentifiable material here and there, the scalp wounds were remarkably clean, and the edges pink and vital, despite the lack of bleeding. It would have been proper to excise the wounds so as to leave fresh surfaces to heal together, but the scalp is notorious for bleeding heavily and it would have been very difficult to cope with that. I decided simply to sew the ragged edges together. Not best practice, but maybe good enough under the circumstances.

After injecting the local anaesthetic at intervals into both edges of the wound that went through her eye and into her nose and picking out the odd bits of dirt and fibres, I set to work. I was completely absorbed now that the decisions were made, and stitched systematically along from the start in her scalp; inserting strong interrupted braided silk sutures right through the scalp, drawing it together. I placed medium sutures for her brow where the strain was less and fine sutures for the eyelid and top of her nose. I left a rubber drain projecting from the wound, to allow any fluids to escape. She was looking better already, though her left eye was a pathetic rag which would have to come out later.

I sewed up the other three wounds in a similar manner. Only one was worrying, because one side of the skull was clearly several millimetres lower than the other, and that could lead to pressure on her brain.

With the help of the nurses, I covered the wounds with gauze swabs, and held wads of sterile cotton wool on top of the swabs while they bandaged them in place. Then, still without a word, this extraordinary young woman climbed off the table and into a wheel chair, so that a porter could take her to the ward where she was put to bed, given antibiotics and a light meal of maize porridge and sweet tea.

The next day she seemed to be perfectly well, but was evidently unable to speak, and a skull X-ray confirmed a depressed fracture over her speech area. This could be the cause of her dumbness, and it might be possible to bring back her speech by levering the bone up again, using the strong side of the skull fracture as a rest for the lever.

When she had been in a week the wounds were healing beautifully, but before removing the stitches I took her back to theatre and removed the shattered eye under general anaesthetic. It could not be left, as the other eye can go blind from sympathetic ophthalmia. It proved a simple matter to grasp the empty globe with toothed locking forceps and cut the strap muscles, and subsequently the optic nerve with curved scissors. I had had to perform a similar operation before, on a man who had had his eye destroyed by a mule kick in the mountains near Qacha's Nek, so I was not surprised by the extraordinary toughness of the optic nerve. I packed the now empty socket with sterile Vaseline tulle and sent the patient back to the ward.

Once again, the damaged socket healed up in record time, but still she could not speak, so it seemed that something had to be done about the depressed fracture.

A week later, her wounds were healing well, so again under general anaesthetic, I made a large curved incision above the offending wound, and turned the scalp down, revealing the depressed fracture. I nibbled the overhanging edge away with bone forceps, but was quite unable to get a purchase to lever up the depressed bone the half a centimetre that would bring it level with the other side. It was jammed tight, so there was nothing for it but to sew her scalp up again, send her back to the ward and hope for the best.

The best happened, probably despite rather than because of my unsuccessful attempt to relieve her depressed fracture. Her speech returned, and one evening, a month after the fateful day of her terrible assault, she walked out of the hospital minus her left eye, but otherwise perfectly well.

I watched the battered truck leave the hospital forecourt and disappear down the street in a swirl of dust. The young woman was sitting in the back, hunched up in her Basuto blanket with a scarf tied round her head. I wondered what she was thinking, and what awaited her at home. Her extraordinary courage, a lot of luck and possibly Divine intervention had helped her recover from the surgery as well as the dreadful assault itself.

Primitive surgery it may have been, but it seemed to have worked well enough this time.

CHAPTER 19
DENTS AND BABIES

A simple skull perforator

The clinic in Maseru took place in a hall close by the hospital. There was so much work to do in the hospital that all the doctors hoped that someone else would have seen the patients who had simply turned up there, some time during the day. The result was that sometimes the last person to leave the hospital was left with a room full of people to see, when all he really wanted to do was to get home for tea and put his feet up. Use of the operating theatre was more or less planned, but everything else simply had to be fitted in, and the patients often had to wait for hours.

"Your turn, Colin, you haven't done the clinic for days," said Adie Lebona. I walked across to the hall and was aghast to find it crammed with people. A quick head count added up to a hundred and five, so there was nothing for it but to sit down with a dispenser and get through them as quickly as possible.

It was quite impossible to do them justice, and indeed most of them only seemed to want a bottle of *mouti* for ill-defined aches and pains, so I simply tried to spot anyone who might have something seriously wrong with them. Two had crackly chests, so I referred them for X-rays, one man looked so ill for no obvious reason that I admitted him to hospital in the hope that it would become clearer when I had more time. Meanwhile regular observations, fluids, a bit of food and good nursing could only help.

"This one looks pretty well," I said to the dispenser, "can you ask his mother what the trouble is?" He was a gorgeous baby, about four months old, with a big smile, well fed and gurgling happily.

"It's his head, *Morena*, his mother is worried about the dent in his head."

Indeed he had a dent in his head, much like the dent you make in a ping-pong ball if you press it hard with your thumb, about an inch and a half across and half an inch deep.

"That's a Pond's fracture," I said. "I've never seen one before, but I have read that you can pull them out somehow. We had better admit him while I go home and read it up. I don't think he is in any danger right now. I'll deal with him in the morning."

That night I pulled down my copy of Hamilton Bailey's *Emergency Surgery* and settled down with a cup of coffee.

"Listen to this, Celia," I said when I had explained about the little baby boy with the dent in his head:

P.D. aged five months was admitted with a depression two inches in diameter in the right parietal region. A few hours previously he had fallen against the knob of an oven door. The infant was anaesthetised. A tiny incision was made over the centre of the depression right down to the bone. The skull was penetrated by a gimlet, and a blunt aneurysm needle was passed. Traction was applied. The depressed area sprang out. One skin suture was all that was necessary to close the wound. Three months later the child was perfectly well and the cranium presented a normal appearance.

Do you think it would work for me?"

"Sounds pretty straightforward; why not have a go?" she replied shovelling some millet porridge into Peter. "All very well for you," I thought "this is a baby we are talking about." I took another look at the book. There was a picture of a baby's head with a dent being pulled out, and another of a gloved hand holding up a gimlet. Underneath it said:

An ordinary carpenter's gimlet with silk wound round to within a quarter of an inch of the point makes a very good perforator. After the silk has been wound the gimlet is sterilised in the usual manner. In a fully equipped hospital I was not able to find an instrument more suited to the purpose.

So the next morning during coffee break I drove down to the store and bought a gimlet, and as I couldn't get hold of any silk, wound cotton round it until there was a fat bulge that should stop me pushing it in too far.

That afternoon, following the instructions to the letter, I gave the gimlet to the theatre nurse to be boiled up. When the baby was anaesthetised and prepared, I cautiously incised the skin in the middle of the dent with the smallest scalpel blade, and stroked down to his skull. His scalp was quite thin and the bone of his skull hard by comparison, so it was not difficult. It hardly bled at all. Now for the gimlet.

I put out my hand. "Gimlet, please," I said, as if I was always asking for such things. The nurse shrugged her shoulders and passed it to me without comment. I took a deep breath, placed the tip in the wound and twisted it gently. Nothing much happened, so with great trepidation I applied a bit more force. The tip began to bite, and after a few more twists I was pretty sure I had made a hole right through. I removed it and passed it to nurse. "Aneurysm needle, please."

An aneurysm needle is a blunt hook with a hole in the end, so that you can pass a thread under a blood vessel easily, but it was only the hook that was required here. At first it would not go into the hole, but after enlarging it with a few more twists of the gimlet, I managed to ease it in, and work it along. I kept it close inside his skull, so that I would not penetrate the *dura mater*, the tough membrane that covers the brain.

Taking a deep breath I gently pulled on the handle, gradually increasing the effort, until, just as the book had predicted, the dent came out, and his head regained its proper shape. I removed the hook, put one stitch into the wound and nurse applied a sterile gauze dressing and bandaged it in place. By the time she had finished, the baby was stirring.

He recovered fully without incident. The only thing Hamilton Bailey forgot, was to tell me to remove the black paint that had been used to prevent the gimlet rusting, and when we took the stitch out there was a tiny black dot where the hole had been. It was probably there for life.

Feeling rather pleased with myself, I was relaxing in the changing room trying to understand the instructions for the electrocardiograph I had persuaded the DMS to buy. Nobody else had a clue how to use the thing. Suddenly the door burst open. "Come quickly doctor, please. There is a baby who is so big that I cannot deliver it. Please hurry." I hurried after the distracted midwife to see what it was all about.

As I drew back the yellow curtains surrounding the bed, I saw a large blue head protruding from between the buttocks of an enormously fat lady. I gave my hands a quick wash and grasped the head firmly and tried to draw it out, a futile gesture really, as doubtless the midwife had tried to do just that, and if she had succeeded, she wouldn't have called me.

The head did not budge, it was wedged tight.

I racked my brains. Impacted shoulders. What on earth did Gibberd say about impacted shoulders? I had never come across them before, but I remembered there was a special manoeuvre for dealing with them, but I couldn't remember what it was. Time was passing. I had to deliver this baby somehow. It was probably too late for the baby, but I still had to deliver it. The moments ticked by.

Then I remembered. It would be the baby's anterior shoulder that was jammed under the mothers pubic symphysis. I managed to insert two fingers behind the baby's head and grasp the elbow of his other arm, the one at the back that wasn't stuck, and hook it out. Then it was relatively simple to rotate the baby until that arm was foremost, and then to hook down the other arm, which was now posterior, in the same way.

"Give her some ergometrine now, nurse, because she is bound to bleed," I said. They always do.

The placenta soon followed, and she only bled a little. The little boy was dead.

I walked shakily back to the rest room and flopped down, pleased to have been able to deliver the child, but sad that I had been unable to save him. A nurse appeared at the door.

"I thought you should know," she said, "that baby weighed fifteen pounds."

"Good heavens," I replied, "no wonder he got stuck. You had better check the mother for diabetes".

There seemed to be no end to the odd obstetrical problems that turned up. Only a few days later a woman went in to labour; there had been no detectable heart beat or movement of the baby for several days. The odd thing was that a small knob just above her pubis hardened whenever she complained of a labour pain, her cervix resolutely refused to open at all, and the baby and all its parts were unusually easy to feel. Eventually she was brought to theatre for a Caesar, and it turned out that the dead baby was fully formed, but outside her uterus, and the placenta which had gone mushy, was attached to practically everything in her lower abdomen. It would have been amazing if we had been able to deliver a live baby, but it was not to be. As it was, she was lucky not to have had a catastrophic bleed.

I was sure that another woman had had an ectopic pregnancy in her left Fallopian tube, but when I opened her up there was no blood to be seen. This was surprising as when I had come across this situation before, the abdomen had been full of blood. In fact in Barbados we used to filter the blood and give it back intravenously.

Before I closed her up again, I felt deep into her left lower abdomen to make sure everything was all right, and my hand sank into a huge crumbly clot. When I had scooped that out I was able to tie off and remove the offending tube with the remains of a very early pregnancy.

That was two near misses. Once again I began to get quite apprehensive about what would turn up next.

CHAPTER 20
REMOVING THINGS

Post mortems can be hard physical work, by the time you have sawn through various bones, taken the top off a skull, and worst of all, removed the thoracic viscera. I never managed to do this with the amazing sleight of hand that marks out the true pathologist. This particular man had died as a result of being crushed by a reversing lorry. His abdomen was full of blood, so when I had sucked it all out, I groped around for his spleen so that I could examine it, and it came to pieces in my hand. That presented me with something of a dilemma; had the spleen ruptured because of the original injury, or as a result of my ham-fistedness? I had never removed a spleen before, so I wasn't sure how strong they ought to be. What was I to put on my report for the coroner's inquest?

After a chewing my pen for a while, I decided that the spleen had been ruptured by the accident. He had clearly died from bleeding into his abdomen, and surely God wouldn't have made an organ so feeble that it came to pieces in my hand.

When I had finished writing up the report, I mused over various matters that were bothering me, and what I had to do in the rest of the day. There was the extraordinary business of Florry Kalaka's defamation. There had never been a moment's trouble in our two years at Qacha's Nek, but the husband of one of the other staff nurses (a delightful man who had been to tea with us) had been accused of defaming Florry in some way, though what Florry could have done which could give rise to the possibility of complaint, I couldn't imagine. I had never met anyone so devoted, hard working and transparent as Florry. The Director of Medical Services considered this to be an important enough issue to down tools and arrange to fly over to attend the hearing, taking his Administrative Secretary and me with him.

It seemed that the defamation had originated as a defamatory letter from a budding politician, which had been translated from Sesuto by the other staff nurse's husband, who had in some way been accused by the same politician of causing the defamation. We were pretty confused by all this, but the staff were vulnerable to criticism and we did not wish them to have to put up with this sort of thing if it was not justified. In the end the hearing was a bit of a farce, because the politician decided to join the other side and speak against himself. Maybe this was a noble gesture, but it was not good for his political credibility. The country was going through strange times, groping towards independence, and politics was breaking out in funny, and sometimes dangerous, ways. We were almost as confused and upset as Florry was by the whole thing, and we all felt much better when the case collapsed.

Another thing on my mind was Education. Norman Salhus, Director of Public Health, and I had been drafted onto the Education Committee to advise on how the Health and Hygeine syllabus for schools in the territory could be improved. What I knew about planning syllabuses was based on having been a pupil at Prep and Public schools in England, which were rather different from State schools in Basutoland. The discussion appeared to run on how many hours a week could be devoted to the topic, and what other subjects would have to be left out if these hours were to be increased.

"What is the evidence that increasing the hours of teaching increases the amount learned?" I asked, innocently. A kind of aghast silence ensued. "Of course it does," said someone after a while. Evidently I had questioned something so fundamental, that they had doubts as to my sanity.

"I was just wondering" I persisted," whether weighing in with a strafe every month or two, perhaps spending a couple of hours doing something relevant that the children would find interesting and could join in with, say, gardening or building a water purification system, would not be more effective than a regular dose of a couple of hours a week. After all it's not a very exciting topic in itself........" I trailed off. I had clearly lost them, and they ignored me thereafter. I did not expect to be invited back, nor was I.

I still had the post-mortem report in my hand, so I sealed it into a buff envelope, and took it across to the DC's office on my way home. I had booked the operating theatre for two o'clock as it looked as if I was going to have to take a bit more off a diabetic man's foot. I had already removed his gangrenous toes and the front third of his foot, but the cut surface was showing no signs of healing; in fact the tissue looked dead.

* * *

"Is leprosy easy to catch?" said Celia over lunch.

"They used to think so in the middle ages. If you were a leper you were completely estranged from society and had to go round ringing a bell and saying *Unclean! Unclean!* so that people could get out of the way,"

I replied.

"Everybody knows that. But you had that little girl with the lion face in an ordinary hospital bed."

That was quite true. Though she didn't look much like a lion, she had the thickened features which gave rise to the description. Leprosy was quite common in Basutoland, and every camp had a leper hut on the outskirts, where visiting lepers were housed, fed, and put on treatment. If they would not come voluntarily, they were fetched by the police.

"Leprosy is caused by a bug similar to the one that causes tuberculosis, and they say it is only transmitted by direct contact with an open leprous sore. It is not like TB which gets into your sputum and you can cough it onto people. Provided they are on treatment and have no open sores, they shouldn't be catching at all. The treatment can't cure the disease, but it can eliminate the bugs that cause it and stop the disease getting any worse." I was beginning to sound like a lecturer. "Why do you want to know?"

"I've heard that there is a Leprosarium a few miles away. Do you think you could take Peter and me out there this evening, so long as you are sure it's safe?" she asked. "It's amazing to think that a disease so mediaeval should still be around, and I wonder what sort of life they have. It must be awful."

"OK. I'm going to have to take a bit more of this chap's leg off first, but I should be back in time for tea."

* * *

Back in theatre after lunch, with the patient asleep on the table, I saw that there was still a major problem with his foot. What was left of it was quite clearly not viable, so I removed it. One look at the footless stump showed that it was not viable either, so I amputated his leg again, this time below the knee, after tying off the arteries. Fortunately he had good tissue there, and I was able to fashion quite a smart stump by pushing the flesh of his leg back before sawing through the bone, so that it flopped down again and could be cut and sewn into a neat cushion.

He recovered remarkably quickly, probably because he had been having chronic pain in his foot, and removing his foot had relieved the pain. He did not appear to be troubled with the phantom pains that often occur after amputation.

There was a man in the next bed to his who had been born with tiny, useless arms, hanging straight down at his sides, yet he could roll and light a cigarette using just his lips and tongue. He had two match boxes, one with tobacco and fragments of paper, and the other with matches. He could open the boxes by holding them in his lips and pushing out the

Topsy

tray with his tongue. Having extracted a piece of paper, he tipped some tobacco into it, rolled up the paper round it and propped it up in the partly open tray. Then he opened the other box, extracted a match, gripped it in his teeth, struck it and applied the flame to the cigarette, hoicked the cigarette out with his tongue and settled back to enjoy the smoke.

It was an extraordinary performance, quite a party trick which he enjoyed showing off to anyone who would stop by.

* * *

Driving to the Leprosarium, which was some miles away across the brown dusty plains out of town, with Peter bouncing up and down on her lap, Celia suddenly said:

"You remember Stephen Howard's dogs that we looked after for a while at Qacha's Nek?

"Of course I do. In fact I came across Patachou the other day. Stephen sold her to some woman who obviously spoils her, and she was as fat as a barrel. She tried to jump up into my arms as she used to when I came home, but she couldn't make it, and hit me at about knee level. She was very pleased to see me, but gone was her slim sportiness. It was quite pathetic." Celia didn't respond for a moment.

"Well, Topsy's dead."

I was stunned. That manic and obsessive fetcher of stones to be thrown, and fetched back again, with the gimlet eyes. "Dead?"

"Apparently Stephen was playing golf. He was just about to drive off when Topsy tried to grab the ball and he could not stop his swing. Killed her instantly."

"What about Larki?"

"He's OK. Still one for the bitches, by all accounts."

Those dogs had given us so much pleasure in our early days at Qacha's Nek. Always on the go and full of fun. They made such a hectic little gang, always rushing round with their tongues hanging out and great grins on their faces. It was sad to think that they would do so no more.

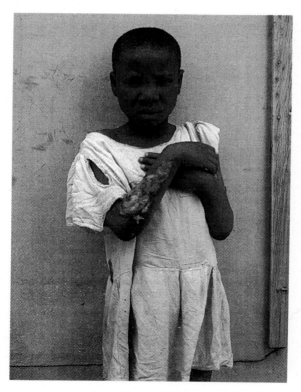

Leper girl

147

The Leprosarium was a cluster of wooden huts, and each leper had his own little room. Mostly they were sitting outside on the *stoep*, making the best of the declining sun. They seemed happy enough despite their deformities. Many had no fingers, as my colleagues used to drive out and snip them off with bone cutting forceps. They could do this without an anaesthetic, because as the leprosy had killed the nerves, the fingers had no feeling and they used to become damaged and horribly infected.

Peter was perfectly happy amongst the lepers, and you could almost feel their love pouring out onto him. He toddled up to one wizened old man, leant on him for support, gave one of his dazzling smiles, and the old man's face lit up with delight. Another smilingly presented me with a picture of Prince Bereng, soon to be Paramount Chief. He had cut it out of a magazine and covered it with a piece of glass on which he had painted a green border, like a frame. I received it as graciously as I could, as that was the proper thing to do, but it did seem a bit odd to be given a present by someone who had nothing

Once again we were astonished by the courage and resignation which we found so often in Basutoland. The Basuto seemed to be able to cope gallantly with levels of deprivation that would have brought us to the brink of suicidal despair.

We drove home in silence.

CHAPTER 21
MOKHOTLONG

Marabaraba board

Some considered Mokhotlong a sort of Outer Mongolia, on the other side of the territory, to which you would be transferred only if you had done something wrong, as it was rather cut off. Others found it rather fascinating. We were sent there for six weeks until a permanent Medical Officer could be found.

The 45 mile track up from Himeville in the Republic traversed the notorious Sani Pass, a series of mad hairpins leading eventually to the Black Mountain, a ghastly bog 10,000 feet up. It was only feasible by courtesy of the Mokhotlong Mountain Transport, a rather ramshackle outfit that had a small fleet of Land Rovers, assembled from those others had thrown away. They prided themselves on getting vehicles with a couple of hundred thousand miles on the clock back into fighting trim.

The last part of the journey was a smoother descent into the camp itself. As we turned the last corner we were amazed to see the Pack Horse Inn awaiting us, a delightful little hotel with a thatched roof and a superb outlook across the valley and a trout stream not far away. A sight that would have graced the prettier parts of Dorset, very refreshing after an exhausting, four hour journey.

There were the usual government offices scattered on the hillside, and a small hospital and dispensary made of grey concrete blocks. There was a lot of greyness about; the rocks were grey, and patients sat around on them in grey blankets playing *marabaraba*, a kind of Nine Men's Morris, with black and white pebbles on a series of concentric squares scratched in the grey rock itself. Such game boards were to be found all over the territory, and the speed with which the game was played, together with the appropriate grunts and shouts, was quite astonishing. They invited me to play with them, but I was hopeless.

The Inn was being run at that time by a bearded Afrikaner called Budkhe. He had two extraordinary boys aged about ten and eleven; they were real children of nature, happy to charge around with nothing on throwing mud at each other. He taught us a bit about how you run a place like the Pack Horse Inn, when practically all food had to come up by Land Rover or pack mule. Nothing could be wasted, and every meal had to incorporate what had been left over from the last, and yet the food had to be attractive and palatable.

The bar was in an attached *rondavel* with a thatched roof. It was quite lively at times, especially with tipsy yarning, from the stream of people passing through and a bunch of lively youngsters who lived somewhere about. One evening a man was talking about lions in the Northern Transvaal and I asked him if he had ever shot one. "Got a left and a right once," said he modestly, that is to say, one with each barrel of his gun. People would argue about who were the toughest and most admirable *Bantu* tribes, and this same man shut us all up by telling us that a *Shangaan* warrior would take on a lion with just a spear, and we were unable to be sure that ours would be quite so foolhardy.

I felt particularly jolly one night and tried to climb up into the roof beams, to the evident fury of our host who hauled me down again. I did redeem myself to some extent by designing a hangover cure to be sold in aid of the Red Cross, consisting of a mixture of bicarbonate of soda and soluble aspirin with a bit of flavouring. It sold well for a while, but had to be withdrawn when it emerged that I was misusing government medicines to make it.

Ntsu (The Eagle) Mokhekhle turned up once. A bull of a man with a shock of black hair, as leader of the revolutionary Congress party he was feared and disliked by people in authority everywhere. He was openly nationalist and supremely confident. He wanted every foreigner out of his country when he took over unless they had a job to do. "Even those Roman Catholic priests can stay as long as they are doing something useful." Twenty years or so later, after various stormy interludes, he was elected prime minister.

* * *

"Can you see my contact lenses anywhere?" said Celia one afternoon after a short sleep. Peter was a year old and into everything by now, and she couldn't find her contact lenses anywhere. We eventually decided that, as Sherlock Holmes once said: *When every other possibility has been eliminated, whatever remains, however absurd, must be the truth,* and so for the next twenty four hours I rinsed the contents of Peter's nappies into a plastic dustbin. I went through the resulting mess in minute detail.

"Found one!" I exclaimed in triumph, when the dustbin was empty except for a few mealie husks. There was no sign of the other lens, but closer inspection I found that they were both there, nestling one inside the other.

On another occasion we found Peter apparently eating the white rings that had been laid by the skirting board to kill cockroaches. When we had tracked down the packet, the instructions inside said that eight of them could kill a man, and we had no idea how many he had eaten. I ran to the hospital and came back with a rubber catheter and a syringe to wash his stomach out with.

"Hold him tight with his head back and his arms down." I said to Celia as I vaselined the catheter and pushed it down his throat. Peter struggled and shouted and vomited the catheter and the contents of his stomach before I could get round to washing him out, so as there was no sign of the crystals in the mess, we decided to leave it at that, and he soon recovered his composure.

As the hospital was quite newly built and the terrain around Mokhotlong extremely mountainous, it was altogether quieter than Qacha's Nek, where people regularly poured in from outlying villages. There were few emergencies, though I did manage to revive one little baby who was dehydrated with gastro-enteritis, by putting a drip in his jugular vein. I did not have the skill, or special needles, to set up a drip in a scalp vein, as I had seen the nurses at Baragwanath hospital do into the fifty or sixty babies they would admit in a day. Each baby was put in a box and shoved along a bench with its drip bottle dangling from an overhead rail. Gastro-enteritis thrived in the shanty towns, and was uncommon out in the countryside.

However there were surprises.

A mother brought her daughter of twenty or so to see me.

"*Morena ngaka,* A bone has grown over my daughter's vagina, please could you remove it," she said, as if this was the most ordinary request in the world.

151

I asked her daughter to climb onto the dispensary couch so that I could have a look, and to my astonishment the entry to her vagina was completely covered by an oval disc, hard and white, that looked extraordinarily like bone. It also was clearly a part of her, as it was continuous with the flesh of the labia minora on either side, and not something that had been introduced. When I pressed it, it gave slightly, rather like when you press a polythene bottle.

"Well, I don't know.....I've never seen anything like this before."

"Please *Morena*. She cannot remain with a bone in her vagina for the rest of her life," said the mother.

So I agreed to have a go. When she was anaesthetised, I carefully incised it down the midline, and found that it was just like cartilage, about an eighth of an inch thick, so feeling my way carefully, I trimmed it away from her vaginal wall. When I examined it closely I decided it was some kind of scar tissue, though how or why it had grown just there I had no idea.

As it was important to keep the raw edges apart to stop them joining together, I had a hock bottle from the hotel sterilised, and she was nursed with the neck inserted as a dilator until the wounds healed, and the raw edges skinned over. I was rather pleased with my handiwork.

"I'm afraid it is not so good, doctor," said the nurse a few days later when I was doing my round. I looked at the young woman, who seemed to be perfectly well.

"What do you mean?" I asked, with a faint feeling of dread.

"She is completely incontinent of urine," she replied.

And so it proved. When she had healed I was able to insert a speculum and take a proper look into the depths of her vagina, where I saw a hole a couple of inches in diameter out of which urine was trickling.

Then things began to make sense. This was a vesico-vaginal fistula, a connection between the bladder and the vagina which comes about as a result of the baby's head crushing the bladder against the back of the pubic bones in a prolonged labour. It is thought to be more likely if the mother is encouraged to try and expel the baby before the cervix is fully dilated, and is quite common in various parts of Africa. They can be repaired by a skilled gynaecological surgeon, but one this big would probably require the construction of an artificial bladder out of a loop of intestine if she was ever to be able to control her urine flow.

The 'bone' across her vagina had gone some way towards solving her problem, just allowing a thin trickle of urine through a tiny hole, over which she seemed to have a measure of control. Now she had no control whatsoever. Another disappointment.

She would have to be flown to Durban to see a real Gynaecological surgeon. Still, maybe I would have saved him the trouble of removing the bone.

About twenty minutes flight from the camp, at over ten thousand feet, there is a sodden hanging valley, called Letseng-le-draai. It was so high that only the Cessnas could land on the bumpy strip; it was too high for the Tri-pacers. The valley was pitted with what looked like small ponds, but were in fact flooded diggings, and was surrounded by hundreds of tiny huts, each about four feet high, with a couple of thousand people living in them. Over the ridge behind the huts, the hillside was largely covered with human excrement.

People survived these appalling conditions, because alluvial diamonds were to be found, if you were lucky, once you had pumped out the water that had filled your hole overnight. It was an impressively ghastly place. The lure of sudden riches was like a drug to both Basuto and the handful of Europeans whom we came across in the hotel in Himeville, dreaming their dreams.

I flew up there every week to hold a clinic, at first in a bell tent, and later in an insulated, prefabricated hut. It made me realise the difference between a bell tent and nothing at all, and the hut seemed like real luxury. There was another hut for the police, who were armed with .303 rifles in case of trouble, as there was a great potential for violence and disorder.

On Black Mountain pass

On one occasion I flew up with the diamond buyer from Jack Scott's company, a subsidiary of de Beer's, and was greatly impressed with his Gladstone bag and automatic pistol. He was in competition with the Illicit Diamond Brokers (IDB), and the diggers didn't know who to take their diamonds to. He offered a standard price from a printed schedule, by weight and water, but once they had produced the diamond it was registered and they had to account for it thereafter. The IDB might have given them a better price, or swapped it for goods they had brought up by mule train, but then they would be breaking the law. The diggers could not tell who would give them the better deal.

To be in possession of an unregistered diamond was a serious crime, punished by imprisonment.

The buyer produced a tiny pair of scales, screwed his magnifier into his eye, and after careful scrutiny and perusing his schedule, quoted a price.

"You see that?" he said, passing me his magnifier. I pushed it into my eye. The diamond looked all right to me. "There, that indented line around the edge? That's what's called a Macle's line. There is a fault running right through the stone."

It was a lovely looking raw diamond of over twenty carats, and the man who brought it was shocked to be offered a poor price because of the fault. If it had been faultless, he would have been lifted out of poverty at a stroke, and his disappointment at finding it worth so little was dreadful to see.

Back in Mokhotlong, there was remarkably little to do in the medical line apart from the usual stream of patients in the dispensaries. The hospital was new, and maybe people hadn't got round to using it. Possibly the terrain was so appalling that people simply died of anything serious before they could reach the hospital, or maybe didn't even bother to try.

Simply trying to get from somewhere to somewhere else in the medical Land Rover-cum-ambulance was exciting, as some of the tracks were scarcely perceptible. Driving along a slippery slope on one occasion, the vehicle simply slid sideways for a hundred yards, completely out of control, until it came to a gentle halt. Celia and I and baby Peter were never nearer death than when all three of us took the Land Rover down the hairpin bends of the Sani pass to Himeville to be serviced. At one point I was driving quite close to the edge to avoid some rocks, when I noticed that one of the coping stones had fallen away, so that in order to reverse away from it, I had to turn the front wheels even closer to the edge. It must have been terrifying for Celia, who could see nothing between us and the next turn of the road fifty feet below, but she simply hugged Peter tighter and awaited the outcome. Perhaps she had absorbed some of the Basuto talent for resignation in the face of fate.

We were beginning to get quite fond of the place once we had adapted to the slower pace of life. There was a stream winding through the bottom of the valley, overhung with the only trees for miles around, and Celia would sit beside it while Peter scrabbled in the sand. Like many of the streams in the Territory it had been stocked with trout and I was learning to cast a wet fly. Whizzing the fly to and fro while letting out line, before finally allowing it to settle on the water, and winding it in again was quite satisfying, provided the fly didn't hook the ground or a branch, even though I never caught anything.

However this was too good to last and in due course it was time to take up our last posting, back in Maseru. In some strange way the surrounding mountains began to seem more and more transparent as the time to leave drew near.

CHAPTER 22
GOING HOME

Horses and mountains

It was a seventeen hour flight from Luanda in Angola to Luxembourg, as practically no country would allow a South African plane to fly over their territory and we had to fly round Africa's mighty western bulge. Celia was dozing beside me and baby Peter was happy enough in a hammock slung between the baggage lockers.

The plane was a slightly battered second hand Super Constellation run by Trek Airways, graceful with its upswept tail of three fins, if a little cramped. I could see the purple flames thundering out of the exhausts of the port inboard engine as I mused on the past three years. I was rather disturbed to see a black oil slick streaked across the wing from one of the engines, but the crew seemed perfectly happy so I presumed it was all right.

I let my mind wander. On the one hand the little mountain kingdom was rapidly taking on the lineaments of a dream, but on the other I could remember practically everything with the utmost clarity and reel it before my mind in vivid colour, as I can still, forty years later. Even as I was fumbling through the extraordinary and often frightening experiences that seemed to rise in front of me like some infernal procession, some of which still haunt me, I must have been scooping up impressions and fastening them in my brain.

Such experiences were like darkling jewels strung here and there in a chaplet of other recollections of quite lyrical beauty, especially of our time at Qacha's Nek. Amongst those beautiful mountains Celia and I had been married and she had given birth to our first child, and now she was expecting another. Her calm common sense and support, especially in my wilder moments, despite the difficulties of a completely unfamiliar situation, had been absolutely crucial. I could see in my mind's eye the stream by which we had sat and silently contemplated the death of her father, who had been ill when she left, and had been unable to come to our wedding. I recalled the waterfall tumbling into a pool in the Sejabatho river which we had tried to climb, and off which I fell on top of her, throwing us both back under water; picnics and making dams with the children of the camp; baby Peter's first paddle on the little beach. So much happiness.

The flow of emotions from anguish to ecstasy as circumstances changed mirrored by the dramatic changes in the weather; from snow, hail and thunderstorms to the limpid clarity of early dawn, the sweet and soothing smell of smouldering dung. The extraordinary courtesy and generosity of the Basuto people with their placid acceptance of the inevitable, tempered by occasional outbursts of violence. The earnest endeavours of the community of government officers, and in particular the District Commissioner, to try and do a good job. The storekeepers who sold everything from a pin to a packsaddle and who were an essential part of the fabric of life in the most inaccessible places.

What a cast of characters we were leaving behind, black and white. Gentle Elsie Kobile with Peter wrapped in a blanket on her back; twinkling Florry Kalaka, staff nurse and midwife; Butler Panyane so calm and precise of speech, without whom I would have been completely lost. A procession of faces, nearly all warm and well-disposed towards us.

Unexpected delights, such as singing Haydn's *Creation* with a Basuto choir, in the village hall over the hill at Qacha's Nek. We were accompanied by a wheezy harmonium, and used the tonic sol-fa in place of music.

My own spiritual journey from patronising, insensitive, self-centred do-gooder, painfully forged into somebody a little more understanding of another world than my own, with most of my attitudes and beliefs challenged, leaving me emotionally battered and in dire need of rest and recuperation.

Eventually I slept too, as we droned on through the night towards whatever future lay ahead.

Forty years on and we live in a different world. The British Empire, which whatever its merits (or lack of merit), consumed so much endeavour from these shores, is almost invisible in the dustbin of history. Basutoland, now called Lesotho, has progressed in this time; there are a few more diamonds coming out, the hydroelectric scheme is in being, and there is an emerging class of bright, well educated youngsters to provide hope for the future. In those days the only tarmac was laid from the railway station at Maseru into the town for a Royal visit some years before, but now many roads have tarmac. However the little country is racked with the sort of political problems that independence brings, and from which it seems to be having great difficulty clawing itself out. The *Pax Britannica* did largely succeed in keeping order when we were there, and letters we have received since independence showed that this security was appreciated by some.

I had had a powerful desire, almost amounting to a compulsion, to serve in Africa for a while. Now it seems a little naive and even childish, but then it seemed like a call, as if my education and training had been leading up to this. I feel more sure now that the need to spare the British taxpayer as much as possible played right into the hands of the owners and shareholders of the gold mines, even if there was no collusion between them and the government at that time. Maybe an endless supply of poorly paid miners to dig out gold away in Johannesburg, with medical care provided by cheap, poorly trained doctors like me, was too good an opportunity to miss, and that people brought up as I had been, to think we were doing our duty, were an economical way of keeping the population reasonably happy despite their poverty.

Governments still seem to be able to justify selling arms to repressive regimes on the grounds that it is good for the economy and keeps people in employment. I think I prefer God, Queen and Country to phoney economics.

But yet, but yet...; that's how it was. We were as we were. Celia and I were married and she bore our first child. The challenges presented to me were the challenges presented; my disasters and successes were just that; the lovely little country and the people we came across, both black and white, who gave us such delight, were as they were. Of course we saw everything through the filters of our own upbringing, and maybe the further filters of time which has passed since then have emphasised the good rather than the dark side, but in this selection of events I have told the tale as truthfully as I can.

We took Peter to see the place of his birth several years later A Korean *Feldscher* had taken my place and the hospital was almost empty; whatever was happening to those throngs of patients who used to besiege the place? We visited Elsie in her scrupulously tidy *rondavel* at Tsoedike mission beyond the stream we had sat beside after Celia's father's death, to show her how her Peter was growing up, which gave her great delight. We gave her a Wedgwood jar, and she gave us a live chicken and a dozen eggs, probably her protein ration for a couple of months. Which was the greater gift?

Some years later she died from her heart trouble, and soon after that Butler Panyane having fathered a number of children, the two eldest of which were called Eric and Celia, was killed in a car crash.

So long ago.